Preparing to Teach
in the Lifelong Learning Sector

Preparing to Teach in the Lifelong Learning Sector

Fourth edition

Ann Gravells

LearningMatters

First published as 'Delivering Adult Learning' in 2006 by Learning Matters Ltd
Reprinted with amendments in 2006
Second edition published in 2007
Reprinted in 2007 (three times)
Third edition published in 2008
Reprinted in 2008 (three times)
Reprinted in 2009 (three times)
Fourth edition published in 2011
Reprinted in 2011

British Library Cataloguing in Publication Data
A CIP record for this book is available from the British Library.

ISBN: 978 0 85725 053 7

This book is available in the following ebook formats:
Adobe ebook ISBN: 9780857250551
EPUB ebook ISBN: 9780857250544
Kindle ISBN: 9780857250568

Cover design by Topics – The Creative Partnership
Project management by Deer Park Productions, Tavistock, Devon
Typeset by PDQ Typesetting Ltd, Newcastle under Lyme
Printed and bound in Great Britain by Bell & Bain Ltd, Glasgow

Learning Matters Ltd
20 Cathedral Yard
Exeter EXI IHB
Tel: 01392 215560
info@learningmatters.co.uk
www.learningmatters.co.uk

Mixed Sources
Product group from well-managed
forests and other controlled sources
www.fsc.org Cert no. TT-COC-002769
© 1996 Forest Stewardship Council
FSC

CONTENTS

5 Enabling learning   72

6 Assessing learning   89

7 Quality assurance and Evaluation   106

8 Micro-teaching   117

Appendices

Index   128

ACKNOWLEDGEMENTS

The author would like to thank the following for their support and encouragement while writing this book.

Peter Adeney
Jennifer Clark
Angela Faulkener
John Fewings
Peter Frankish
Bob Gravells
Gaynor Mount
Susan Simpson
Amy Thornton
Jacklyn Williams

The staff and learners of the Teacher Training Department at Bishop Burton College, who always inspire the author.

All readers of previous editions of this book who have taken the time to give feedback. This has been extremely valuable and has greatly helped the author to restructure and focus the content towards the specific PTLLS assessment criteria.

Every effort has been made to trace the copyright holders and to obtain their permission for the use of copyright material. The publisher and author will gladly receive any information enabling them to rectify any error or omission in subsequent editions.

Ann Gravells is a lecturer in teacher training at Bishop Burton College in East Yorkshire. She has been teaching since 1983.

She is a consultant to City & Guilds for various projects as well as externally verifying the City & Guilds teacher training qualifications.

Ann holds a Masters in Educational Management, a PGCE, a Degree in Education, and a City & Guilds Medal of Excellence for teaching.

Ann is a Fellow of the Institute for Learning and holds QTLS status.

She is the author of:

- *Principles and Practice of Assessment in the Lifelong Learning Sector*
- *Delivering Employability Skills in the Lifelong Learning Sector*
- *Passing PTLLS Assessments.*

She is co-author of:

- *Planning and Enabling Learning in the Lifelong Learning Sector*
- *Equality and Diversity in the Lifelong Learning Sector*
- *Passing CTLLS Assessments.*

She has edited:

- *Study Skills for PTLLS.*

The author welcomes any comments from readers; please contact her via her website.

Website – **www.anngravells.co.uk**

In this chapter you will learn about:

- the structure of the book and how to use it;
- teaching in the Lifelong Learning Sector;
- Lifelong Learning professional teaching standards;
- The Institute for Learning.

The structure of the book and how to use it

Congratulations upon making the decision to become a teacher in the Lifelong Learning Sector. You might be working towards a teaching qualification or just want to find out what it's like to be a teacher. This book will give you the information you need to set you on your learning journey. It has been written with new teachers in mind, in a language which is not full of educational jargon. This book will act as a good introduction to teaching in the Lifelong Learning Sector; however, you may also wish to refer to the websites and texts listed at the end of each chapter to inform your learning further.

The book is structured in chapters which relate to the full process of teaching and learning often referred to as the training cycle or teaching and learning cycle. The chapters cover the content of the PTLLS Award at level 3 and level 4.

There are five learning outcomes which you will need to successfully evidence to achieve the PTLLS Award.

1. Understand own role, responsibilities and boundaries of role in relation to teaching.
2. Understand appropriate teaching and learning approaches in the specialist area.
3. Demonstrate session planning skills.
4. Understand how to deliver inclusive sessions which motivate learners.
5. Understand the use of different assessment methods and the need for record keeping.

The content of the learning outcomes is the same at both level 3 and level 4; the difference in level is expressed in the amount of work you will be required to submit. For example, if you are taking level 3, you will *explain* how or why you do something; at level 4 you will *analyse* how or why you do it. If you are working towards level 4, you will need to carry out relevant research, reference your work to theorists and use an academic style of writing. Further information and guidance regarding academic writing and research are available in the companion book *Study Skills for PTLLS* by Jacklyn Williams.

You can work logically through the book by starting with Chapter I or you can just look up appropriate topics in the index to access aspects relevant to your current study. There are activities to enable you to think about how you teach, examples to help you understand the process of teaching and learning and extension activities to develop, stretch and challenge your learning further. While this book covers the theory required for the PTLLS Award, the companion book *Passing PTLLS Assessments* by Ann Gravells will help you put theory into practice and structure your evidence to meet the learning outcomes.

Each chapter is cross-referenced to the overarching *Professional Standards for Teachers, Tutors and Trainers in the Lifelong Learning Sector*. Throughout this book, the generic term *teacher* is used, even though you might be called something different; for example, *assessor, facilitator, instructor, lecturer, trainer* or *tutor*. The generic term *learner* is also used and refers to other terms such as *apprentice, candidate, participant, pupil, student* or *trainee*.

If you are teaching nationally or internationally, some of the regulations and organisations referred to in the book may only be relevant in England. You are therefore advised to check what is current and applicable to the nation or country in which you work.

The appendices contain the PTLLS Award learning outcomes and assessment criteria at level 3 and level 4. There is also a useful teaching and learning checklist.

Teaching in the Lifelong Learning Sector

Teaching is about helping someone reach their full potential, whether this is for personal or professional reasons. The Lifelong Learning Sector can include learners from age 14 upwards, therefore you have the opportunity to help make a difference to someone's life and career, which can be very rewarding. If you are new to teaching, this could be because you are contemplating a change of profession or you are required to take a particular teaching qualification because of your job role. Perhaps you have a hobby or a trade you would like to teach others; you know you are good at it and feel you have the experience and knowledge which you could pass on to others. While this book will guide you through the process of teaching and learning, it is up to you to ensure you are current with your subject knowledge. Depending upon where and what you are going to teach, you may not need to be qualified in your particular subject, but be able to demonstrate appropriate experience and knowledge at a particular level.

The most important aspect of teaching is to ensure that learning is taking place. If you are currently teaching, your delivery methods might be based on experiences of how you were taught in the past. However, there are many teaching and learning approaches you could use and this book will hopefully give you new ideas to teach in a more professional and inclusive manner. Teaching isn't just about delivering to groups in a classroom; it can take place in many different environments such as the workplace, public, private or voluntary settings, outdoors, or online via the internet.

Lifelong Learning professional teaching standards

In September 2007, standards came into effect for all new teachers in the Lifelong Learning Sector who teach on government-funded programmes in England. This includes all post-16 education, including further education, adult and community learning, work-based learning and offender education. Please see the web links at the end of the chapter for Northern Ireland, Scotland and Wales.

The key purpose of the teacher is to create effective and stimulating opportunities for learning through high-quality teaching that enables the development and progression of all learners. Teachers in the Lifelong Learning Sector should value all learners individually and equally. They are committed to lifelong learning and professional development and strive for continuous improvement through reflective practice.

The full standards encompass six domains.

A   Professional values and practice

B   Learning and teaching

C   Specialist learning and teaching

D   Planning for learning

E   Assessment for learning

F   Access and progression

The chapters in this book are cross-referenced to these domains; however, the standards are incorporated into the following qualifications.

- Preparing to Teach in the Lifelong Learning Sector (PTLLS)
- Certificate in Teaching in the Lifelong Learning Sector (CTLLS)
- Diploma in Teaching in the Lifelong Learning Sector (DTLLS)

All new teachers must undertake the Preparing to Teach in the Lifelong Learning Sector (PTLLS) Award at the beginning of their career. This can be as a discrete Award or embedded in the Certificate or Diploma. Higher education institutions can still use the terms *Certificate in Education* and *Postgraduate* or *Professional Certificate in Education*. However, the content is the same as the Diploma, but it may be offered at a higher level. See Chapter 7 for details regarding progression from PTLLS, as the next qualification you take (either CTLLS or DTLLS) is dependent solely upon your job role as a teacher.

As you progress through the teaching qualifications, you will need to meet all the relevant criteria relating to the scope, knowledge and practice required in your job role (referenced by: S for scope, K for knowledge or P for practice within the chapters).

The qualifications have been developed based upon the Qualifications and Credit Framework (QCF) model which has mandatory and optional units at different levels with different credit values. The units and credits can be built up to form relevant qualifications over time. The teaching qualifications start at level 3 on the QCF and can be obtained through an Awarding Organisation (AO) or Higher Education Institute (HEI).

The Institute for Learning

The Institute for Learning (IfL) is the professional body for teachers, trainers, tutors and trainee teachers in the Learning and Skills Sector. Teachers should register with the IfL and follow a Code of Professional Practice (2008) along with the associated disciplinary processes. If you haven't already done so, you will need to register with the IfL via their website, **www.ifl.ac.uk**.

While working towards your PTLLS Award, it would be extremely beneficial for you to have a mentor, someone who can help and support you, not only with teaching skills, but also with your specialist subject. Your mentor could observe you teaching and give you developmental feedback; conversely, you could observe them to gain useful ideas and tips for teaching and learning.

Summary

In this chapter you have learnt about:

- the structure of the book and how to use it;
- teaching in the Lifelong Learning Sector;
- Lifelong Learning professional teaching standards;
- The Institute for Learning.

Theory focus
References and further information

Gravells, A (2010) *Passing PTLLS Assessments*. Exeter Learning Matters.
IfL (2008) *Code of Professional Practice: Raising concerns about IfL members*. London: Institute for Learning.
LLUK (2006) *New Overarching Professional Standards for Teachers, Tutors and Trainers in the Lifelong Learning Sector*. London: LLUK.
Williams, J (2010) *Study Skills for PTLLS*. Exeter: Learning Matters.

Websites

Ann Gravells (information regarding teaching qualifications)
— www.anngravells. co.uk
Further Education Teachers' Qualifications (England) Regulations (2007)
— www. legislation.gov.uk/uksi/2007/2264/contents/made

Further Education Teachers' Qualifications (Wales) – http://tiny.cc/ol0oc
Institute for Learning – www.ifl.ac.uk
Lifelong Learning UK – www.lluk.org
Professional Standards for Lecturers in Scotland – http://tiny.cc/3w9jg
Qualifications and Credit Framework – www.qca.org.uk/qualifications/6/.aspx
Teaching Qualifications for Northern Ireland – http://tiny.cc/dq2dg

Introduction

In this chapter you will learn about:

- roles and responsibilities of a teacher;
- boundaries of teaching;
- record keeping;
- legislation and codes of practice.

There are activities and examples to help you reflect on the above which will assist your understanding of the process of teaching and learning. There are extension activities to stretch and challenge your learning further.

This chapter contributes towards the following scope, knowledge and practice aspects of the Professional Standards for Teachers, Tutors and Trainers in the Lifelong Learning Sector:

AS1, AS6, AS7, AK2.1, AK2.2, AK4.2, AK6.1, AK6.2, AK7.1, AK7.2, AP6.1, AP6.2, AP7.1;
BS2, BK1.3, BK2.7, BP2.7;
CS1, CS3, CS4, CK1.1, CK1.2, CK4.1, CP1.1;
FS2, FK2.1, FP2.1.

Roles and responsibilities of a teacher

Most careers are quite challenging and demanding, and teaching is no exception to this. However, it can be very rewarding when you see your learners' achievements and success, which is a direct result of your contribution. Your main role as a teacher should be to teach your subject in a way that actively involves and engages your learners during every session. You should use clear language at an appropriate level and in terms they will understand, motivating them to want to learn more. You should also manage the learning process from when your learners commence to when they complete, ensuring you assess their progress, give relevant feedback and keep appropriate records.

How you do this will depend upon your subject, the age and experience of your learners and the environment you will teach in. Becoming a good teacher includes being enthusiastic and passionate about your subject, being approachable and taking pride in your work, which will all be conveyed to your learners through your teaching approaches.

Example

Zak always arrives early to his sessions, he ensures the room is tidy and organises the tables and chairs in a way that encourages communication. He creates an approachable environment and delivers his subject with passion and enthusiasm. He uses lots of examples and anecdotes to relate his subject to real life. He includes all his learners by addressing them personally, yet remains fair with the support and advice he gives. He always tidies up afterwards and e-mails additional learning materials as required. His learners see how conscientious and professional Zak is and begin to emulate this by being early, being polite and submitting work on time.

A good first impression will help establish a positive working relationship with your learners. The way you dress, act, respond to questions, offer support, etc., will also influence your learners. They don't need to know anything personal about you, but they will probably make assumptions about you. If asked personal questions, try not to give out any information: by remaining a professional, and not becoming too friendly, you will retain their respect. Establishing routines will help your sessions flow smoothly; for example, always starting on time, setting and keeping to time limits for activities and breaks, and finishing on time.

The teaching and learning cycle

The teaching and learning cycle is so called as it can start at any stage and keep on going. However, all stages must be addressed for teaching and learning to be effective. The chapters in this book are based on the cycle, which consists of the stages outlined in Figure 1.1 below.

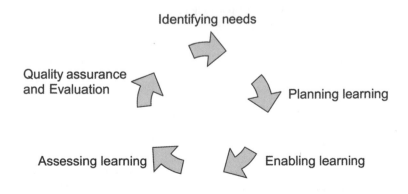

Figure 1.1 The teaching and learning cycle

Your role will usually follow the cycle and briefly involve:

- identifying needs – finding out what your organisation's, your own, and potential learners' needs are, carrying out initial assessments, agreeing individual learning plans;

- planning learning – preparing a scheme of work, session plans and teaching and learning materials to ensure you cover the requirements of the syllabus, liaising with others;

- enabling learning – teaching and facilitating learning using a variety of approaches;

- assessing learning – checking your learners have gained the necessary skills and knowledge;

- quality assurance and evaluation – obtaining feedback from others, evaluating yourself and the programme in order to make improvements for the future. Evaluation should also be an ongoing process throughout all stages of the cycle.

Most teachers follow the cycle from beginning to end; however, your job role might not require you to be involved with all aspects. You will probably undertake a variety of roles during your teaching career, each having various responsibilities or duties that you must carry out. The job roles do not relate to whether you are employed full-time or part-time, but to the duties you will perform. Lifelong Learning UK (LLUK) has identified two teaching roles in the further education sector in England.

- Associate teaching role which has fewer teaching responsibilities and will be performed by those who are expected to gain the status of Associate Teacher, Learning and Skills (ATLS). An Associate Teacher will usually teach using materials prepared by others.

- Full teaching role which represents the full range of responsibilities performed by those who are expected to gain the status of Qualified Teacher, Learning and Skills (QTLS). A Full Teacher will follow all aspects of the teaching and learning cycle.

Table 1.1 on page 9 lists examples of teaching roles and responsibilities, based on the teaching and learning cycle. Don't be concerned by the amount of detail in the table; your job role might not require you to carry them all out. If there is anything you are unsure of at the moment, as you progress through the book it should all become clear.

To teach effectively involves not only the approaches you use to teach your subject, but many other factors that go before and after the taught session. This includes planning your sessions, preparing your teaching materials, assessing your learners, marking work, giving feedback and evaluating yourself and the experience your learners have.

Your personality and mannerisms will be noticed by your learners. You may do things you are not aware of; for example, waving your arms around or fidgeting. It is really useful to make a visual recording of one of your sessions to enable you to watch yourself afterwards. You may see things you didn't realise you did or things that you would like to change.

Table 1.1 Examples of teaching roles and responsibilities

Roles	Responsibilities
Identifying needs	
<ul><li>arranging for suitable initial assessments to take place; for example, to ascertain current skills and knowledge;</li><li>carrying out interviews with learners;</li><li>identifying any barriers or challenges to learning;</li><li>identifying any particular learner, self and organisational needs;</li><li>identifying learning styles;</li><li>knowing the boundaries within which to work;</li><li>participating in recruitment activities.</li></ul>	<ul><li>attending promotional events to publicise the programme;</li><li>dressing appropriately;</li><li>ensuring learners are on the right programme;</li><li>following organisational policies and procedures;</li><li>giving appropriate information, advice and guidance;</li><li>helping learners arrange funding/grants;</li><li>keeping records of what was discussed and agreed;</li><li>maintaining confidentiality;</li><li>referring learners to other people or agencies when necessary;</li><li>registering with the Institute for Learning (IfL);</li><li>undertaking a Criminal Records Bureau (CRB) check.</li></ul>
Planning learning	
<ul><li>planning what will be taught and when;</li><li>preparing teaching and learning resources and activities.</li></ul>	<ul><li>agreeing individual learning plans;</li><li>carrying out risk assessments;</li><li>creating a safe, positive and accessible learning environment for learners and visitors;</li><li>designing a scheme of work, session plans and appropriate materials and resources;</li><li>having a contingency plan in place;</li><li>liaising with others;</li><li>obtaining the relevant syllabus or qualification handbook;</li><li>writing realistic aims.</li></ul>
Enabling learning	
<ul><li>carrying out tutorial reviews;</li><li>communicating appropriately and effectively;</li><li>conforming to professional codes of practice and values;</li><li>embedding functional skills;</li><li>establishing ground rules;</li><li>following awarding organisation and external body requirements;</li><li>inducting learners to the organisation and programme;</li><li>maintaining a duty of care towards your learners;</li><li>teaching in an inclusive and engaging way;</li></ul>	<ul><li>acting and speaking appropriately;</li><li>acting professionally and with integrity;</li><li>being qualified/experienced to teach your subject;</li><li>carrying out administrative requirements;</li><li>completing attendance records;</li><li>dealing with behaviour issues as they occur;</li><li>differentiating teaching and learning materials and approaches;</li><li>engaging and encouraging learning;</li><li>following health and safety, equality and diversity, safeguarding requirements and relevant legislation and codes of practice;</li><li>knowing who the appointed first aider is;</li></ul>

Enabling learning *continued*	
• using a variety of teaching and learning approaches to motivate learners; • using icebreakers and energisers effectively.	• following professional values and ethics; • following up absences; • helping and supporting learners as appropriate; • incorporating new technology; • keeping records of what has been taught and to whom; • keeping up to date with developments relating to your subject; • maintaining a professional relationship with learners; • not forcing your own attitudes, values and beliefs upon your learners; • tidying the area after each session; • using appropriate equipment and resources; • using appropriate teaching and learning approaches.
Assessing learning	
• assessing progress; • following awarding organisation and external body requirements.	• assessing work within an agreed time period; • checking for plagiarism if applicable; • ensuring decisions are valid, reliable, fair and ethical; • giving feedback to learners; • informing learners of their right to appeal; • keeping records of individual achievements; • maintaining confidentiality; • preparing realistic assessment materials; • standardising decisions with others; • using a variety of assessment methods: initial, formative, summative, formal and informal.
Quality assurance and Evaluation	
• evaluating how well the programme was planned and delivered; • improving the teaching and learning process.	• attending meetings; • encouraging learner development and progression; • encouraging ongoing feedback from learners and others; • evaluating each session you taught, along with the teaching and learning approaches and materials used; • helping learners achieve their full potential; • liaising with others, e.g. external verifiers and inspectors; • maintaining own professional development and subject currency; • partaking in organisational quality assurance processes; • standardising practice with others.

If you are new to teaching, you may find you are teaching in the same way you were taught at school or college. This could be lecturing, reading from a book or writing information on a board, which might not have been very effective for you. You won't yet know all the other methods you could use to make learning interesting and engaging. Active learning helps people remember; passive learning may lead them to forget. As you become more experienced at teaching, your confidence will grow and you will be able to experiment with different approaches, as not all teaching methods suit all learners.

Activity

Think about the subject you would like to teach, the age group of your learners and the environment in which you will teach. What do you consider your roles and responsibilities will be to ensure learning is effective? If you are in-service, compare your responses with your job description.

Boundaries of teaching

You will have professional boundaries within which to work and it's important not to overstep these by becoming too personal with your learners. Boundaries are about knowing where your role as a teacher stops and working within the limits of that role.

Example

Navinda had been teaching a group of 16 learners once a week for six weeks. She occasionally e-mailed them between sessions to inform them of room changes. Two of her learners sent her an e-mail inviting her to join their social networking site. She politely refused, to ensure that she remained professional in her role as their teacher.

You need to remain in control, be fair and ethical with all your learners and not demonstrate any favouritism towards particular learners; for example, by giving one more support than the others. You might feel it sensible to make a telephone call to a learner who has been absent but making regular calls would be inappropriate. Giving your personal telephone number to learners could be seen as encouraging informal contact, and you may get calls or texts which are not suitable or relevant. You might not want to take your break with your learners or join their social networking sites as you could become more of a friend than a teacher. It is unprofessional to use bad language, to touch learners in an inappropriate way or to let your personal problems affect your work. Boundaries also include the constraints you might be under as a teacher; for example, the amount of paperwork you are expected to complete or the lack of funding or resources. Boundaries can often be interpreted as the negative aspects to your roles and responsibilities.

Table 1.2 Boundaries of teaching

Identifying needs	<ul><li>demands from managers;</li><li>expectations of learners;</li><li>funding constraints;</li><li>knowing what advice and/or information can and cannot be given to learners;</li><li>lack of information regarding learners' requirements;</li><li>learners not at the required starting level;</li><li>negative culture within a department or organisation;</li><li>organisational policies, procedures and administrative requirements;</li><li>requirements of codes of practice, awarding organisations and external bodies;</li><li>standards and levels learners are expected to achieve.</li></ul>
Planning learning	<ul><li>capability of learners to achieve;</li><li>equality and diversity policies;</li><li>financial concerns – organisation and learners;</li><li>health and safety regulations;</li><li>lack of access to computers and technology-based learning materials;</li><li>lack of adequate equipment and access to resources, e.g. photocopying;</li><li>not enough knowledge of individual learners and their learning styles;</li><li>requirements of, or a lack of understanding of the syllabus or qualification requirements;</li><li>unsupportive colleagues.</li></ul>
Enabling learning	<ul><li>ability of learners, e.g. lack of English;</li><li>barriers to learning such as access, or lack of specialist equipment and resources;</li><li>behaviour issues;</li><li>broken or faulty equipment and resources;</li><li>changes in legislation, codes of practice, policies and procedures;</li><li>deadlines and targets;</li><li>disruptive learners;</li><li>inability to be flexible when teaching, to take into account needs of learners;</li><li>inappropriate actions of self or learners;</li><li>inappropriate seating or working areas;</li><li>lack of a suitable environment and/or resources;</li><li>lack of own subject knowledge;</li><li>learners' lack of motivation, demands or high expectations;</li><li>learners' personal and welfare issues;</li><li>not enough time for teaching and learner support;</li><li>not hindering an individual's progress just because they are learning quicker than the group;</li><li>own personal problems;</li><li>requirements of relevant legislation, e.g. risk assessments;</li><li>safeguarding requirements.</li></ul>
Assessing learning	<ul><li>data protection and confidentiality;</li><li>demands of paperwork and administration;</li><li>meeting deadlines and targets;</li><li>not being biased or unfair with judgements;</li><li>not enough evidence from learners to make a decision;</li><li>not giving some learners more support than others;</li><li>not passing learners just to achieve your targets;</li><li>objectivity when making decisions.</li></ul>
Quality assurance and Evaluation	<ul><li>awarding organisation's demands, e.g. internal and external verification;</li><li>lack of time to attend training events, standardisation activities, CPD or meetings;</li><li>organisation's targets and demands;</li><li>own ability to listen to and react to feedback.</li></ul>

Extension Activity

What boundaries do you think you will encounter as a teacher and why? How can you effectively overcome them and who would you go to for support and advice?

Table I.2 on page I2 lists some of the boundaries you may encounter in relation to the teaching and learning cycle.

Record keeping

Records must be maintained, not only to support the teaching and learning process, but to satisfy auditors, inspectors, regulators, verifiers and your own organisation's requirements. For example, information and data gathering can inform quality assurance, equality and diversity, and health and safety policies. The information contained in records helps to measure learning and the effectiveness and appropriateness of the programme overall. Information such as attendance, progress and achievement could be shared with your colleagues if they are also teaching your learners; for example, to look for patterns of attendance or behaviour issues. If accurate records are not maintained, your learners' progress may become unstructured and their achievement may not be recognised or recorded.

Records must be up to date, accurate, factual and legible whether they are stored manually or electronically. All records should show an audit trail, i.e. track learner progress from when they commenced through to their completion. If you happen to be absent for any reason, a colleague will be able to effectively take over if they have access to your records. Data are also useful to your organisation for purposes such as accidents, appeals, equal opportunities and funding purposes.

Example

Nick has set up a file which contains all the documentation relevant to deliver and assess the Certificate in Sport and Recreation. This includes a hard copy of the syllabus, scheme of work, session plans, and teaching and learning materials. He also has a file which contains alphabetical records relating to each of his learners. This includes application forms, interview notes, initial assessment results, action plans, tutorial review records and assessment results. These files ensure he has everything to hand, not only to carry out his role effectively, but also for auditors, inspectors and verifiers.

Try and keep on top of your paperwork, even if this is carried out electronically. If you leave it for a while, you may forget to note, sign or date important details.

Table 1.3 Records

Identifying needs	• application forms; • diagnostic test results; • enrolment forms; • initial assessment results; • interview notes; • learner contract; • learning style results; • learning support records; • personal details of learners, e.g. address, contacts, disabilities; • syllabus or qualification handbook; • targets and funding data; • unique learner numbers (ULN).
Planning learning	• individual learning plans/action plans; • risk assessments; • scheme of work; • session plans; • timetables.
Enabling learning	• accident/incident forms; • agreed ground rules; • attendance records/registers; • details of learner progress and behaviour; • disciplinary records; • evidence of embedding equality and diversity, functional skills and Every Child/Learner Matters; • induction records; • records of what was taught; • tutorial review records.
Assessing learning	• achievement and success data; • assessment plans; • awarding organisation registration numbers; • feedback records and decisions/grades (initial, formative and summative); • receipts for the submission and return of assignments; • tracking sheets; • see *Chapter 6 for a full list of assessment records.*
Quality assurance and Evaluation	• complaints and appeals; • continuing professional development records; • equal opportunities data; • inspection reports; • internal and external verification reports; • minutes of meetings; • questionnaire and feedback analysis; • retention and achievement data; • standardisation records.

Records should be kept confidential and secure at your organisation; for example, in a locked filing cabinet. The Data Protection Act (1998 amended 2003) is mandatory for all organisations that hold or process personal data. It contains eight principles, to ensure that data are:

- processed fairly and lawfully;
- obtained and used only for specified and lawful purposes;
- adequate, relevant and not excessive;
- accurate, and where necessary, kept up to date;
- kept for no longer than necessary;
- processed in accordance with the individual's rights;
- kept secure;
- transferred only to countries that offer adequate protection.

Extension Activity

Make a list of the records you should maintain and explain why you need to keep them. If you are in-service, find out from your mentor what the exact requirements of your organisation are and where and for how long you should keep records.

Table 1.3 on page 14 lists some of the records you might keep, in relation to the teaching and learning cycle.

Legislation and codes of practice

It is important for you to keep up to date with all relevant legislation and codes of practice to ensure you are remaining current with your knowledge and practice, and any changes or updates that have taken place. These can be grouped into generic, i.e. relating to your role as a teacher, and specific, i.e. relating to your specialist subject.

Generic

These will differ depending upon the context and environment within which you teach. You need to be aware of the requirements of external bodies and regulators such as Ofsted (in England) who inspect provision, along with awarding organisations who will quality-assure their qualifications, and funding agencies who will need data and statistics. Your own organisation will have relevant codes of practice such as disciplinary, conduct, dress, timekeeping and sustainability. There will also be policies and procedures to follow such as appeals, complaints, and risk assessments etc. If you are employed, you will have received a contract of employment and employee handbook which should state your organisation's rules and procedures.

The following information was current at the time of writing; however, you are advised to check for any changes or updates, and whether they are applicable outside England.

Examples of generic legislation and codes of practice are as follows.

- Children Act (2004): Every Child Matters provided the legal underpinning for the Every Child Matters: Change for Children programme and is covered in more detail in Chapter 5. 'Well-being' is the term used in the Act to define the five Every Child Matters outcomes, which are:
  - be healthy;
  - stay safe;
  - enjoy and achieve;
  - make a positive contribution;
  - achieve economic well-being.

- Code of Professional Practice (2008) introduced by the Institute for Learning (IfL) to cover the activities of teachers in the Lifelong Learning Sector. The Code is based on seven behaviours, namely:
  - professional integrity;
  - respect;
  - reasonable care;
  - professional practice;
  - criminal offence disclosure;
  - responsibility during Institute investigations;
  - responsibility.

- Copyright Designs and Patents Act (1988) relates to the copying, adapting and distributing of materials, which includes computer programs and materials found via the internet. Your organisation may have a licence to enable you to photocopy small amounts from books or journals. Anything you do copy should be acknowledged.

- Data Protection Act (1998 amended 2003) made provision for the regulation of the processing of information relating to individuals, including the obtaining, holding, use or disclosure of such information. The amendment included electronic data.

- Disability Discrimination Act (DDA) (1995 amended 2005) required that all learners must be given the necessary adaptations to allow them to fully participate in their learning. The Special Educational Needs and Disability Act (SENDA) (2001) amended the DDA to bring education specifically within its remit. Now included in the Equality Act 2010.

- Education and Skills Act (2008) aimed to increase participation in learning for young people and adults. It puts in place a right for adults to basic and intermediate skills, giving adults a second chance to gain the skills they need to thrive in society and throughout their working lives.

- Employment Equality (Religion or Belief) Regulations (2003) are to protect workers, including those on vocational training programmes, from discriminatory employment practices based on actual or perceived religion, or similar belief defined as religion, religious belief or similar philosophical belief.

- Employment Equality (Sexual Orientation) Regulations (2003) are to protect workers, including those on vocational training programmes, from discriminatory employment practices based on actual or perceived sexual orientation defined as heterosexual, gay, lesbian or bisexual.

- Equality Act (2006) replaced the Equal Opportunities Commission (EOC), the Commission for Racial Equality (CRE) and the Disability Rights Commission (DRC). The Act aims to eliminate discrimination, reduce inequality, protect human rights and to build good relations, ensuring that everyone has a fair chance to participate in society. This Act is covered in more detail in Chapter 3. The Act covers the six strands:
  - age;
  - disability;
  - gender;
  - race;
  - religion and belief;
  - sexual orientation.

- Equality Act (2010) brings disability, sex, race and other grounds of discrimination within one piece of legislation.

- Freedom of Information Act (2000) gives learners the opportunity to request to see the information your organisation holds about them.

- Health and Safety at Work Act (1974) imposes obligations on all staff within an organisation commensurate with their role and responsibility. Risk assessments should be carried out where necessary. In the event of an accident, particularly one resulting in death or serious injury, an investigation by the Health and Safety Executive may result in the prosecution of individuals found to be negligent as well as the organisation.

- Human Rights Act (1998) gives all people basic rights. All public bodies are required to adhere to the Act and the courts must interpret UK law in accordance with the European Convention on Human Rights and Fundamental Freedoms.

- Protection of Children Act (POCA) (1999) was designed to protect children. It gives responsibility to local authorities to make enquiries when anyone contacts them with concerns about child abuse. You will need to be checked by the Criminal Records Bureau (CRB) if you are teaching children or vulnerable adults.

- Safeguarding Vulnerable Groups Act (2006) introduced a vetting and barring scheme to make decisions about who should be barred from working with children and vulnerable adults. You may need to have a CRB check before you can teach.

- Sex Discrimination Act (1975) made it illegal to treat a woman or a man less favourably on the grounds of their sex or marital status. Now included in the Equality Act (2010).

- Race Relations Act (1976 amended 2000) made it illegal to discriminate on grounds of colour, race, nationality, ethnic or national origins. Now included in the Equality Act (2010).

- The Further Education Teachers' Qualifications (England) Regulations (2007) brought in revised teaching qualifications for new teachers and a professional status for all teachers in the further education sector in England. Teachers must register with the Institute for Learning (IfL) and partake in continuing professional development (CPD). Teachers should be qualified and hold QTLS or ATLS status within five years of taking a teaching position. See 'Progression' in Chapter 7 for further details.

Specific

These will differ depending upon the subject and environment within which you teach. Examples of specific legislation and codes of practice are as follows.

- Control of Substances Hazardous to Health (COSHH) Regulations (2002) if you work with hazardous materials.

- Food Hygiene Regulations (2006) apply to aspects of farming, manufacturing, distributing and retailing food.

- Information Technology Codes of Practice relate to the use of computers in your particular organisation; for example, internet access and e-mail protocol.

- Management of Health and Safety at Work Regulations (1999) aims to prevent unsafe practices and minimise risks; for example, the use of visual displays.

- Manual Handling Operation Regulations (1992) relate to hazards of manual handling and risks of injury.

- Reporting of Injuries, Diseases and Dangerous Occurrences (RIDDOR) Regulations (1995) – specified workplace incidents must be reported.

Following the required legislation and codes of practice, and carrying out your roles and responsibilities to the best of your ability will help ensure you become an effective and professional teacher.

Extension Activity

Identify and research the legislation and codes of practice relevant to your subject area and the context/environment within which you will teach. Summarise the key aspects of these and state how they could impact upon your role.

Summary

In this chapter you have learnt about:

- roles and responsibilities of a teacher;

- boundaries of teaching;

- record keeping;

- legislation and codes of practice.

Theory focus

References and further information

Francis M and Gould J (2009) *Achieving your PTLLS Award*. London: Sage Publications Ltd.

IfL (2008) *Code of Professional Practice*. London: Institute for Learning.

LLUK (2006) *New Overarching Professional Standards for Teachers, Tutors and Trainers in the Lifelong Learning Sector*. London: Skills for Business.

HMI (2004) *Every Child Matters: Change for Children*. London: DfES.

Reece, I and Walker, S (2008) *Teaching Training and Learning: A practical guide* (6th edn). Tyne & Wear: Business Education Publishers Ltd.

Tummons, J (2010) *Becoming a Professional Tutor in the Lifelong Learning Sector* (2nd edn). Exeter: Learning Matters.

Wilson, L (2008) *Practical Teaching: A Guide to PTLLS and CTLLS*. London: Cengage Learning.

Websites

All government legislation and regulations – www.opsi.gov.uk

Criminal Records Bureau – www.crb.gov.uk

Institute for Learning – www.ifl.ac.uk

Lifelong Learning UK (LLUK) – www.lluk.org.uk

Office for Standards in Education – www.ofsted.gov.uk

2 THEORIES OF LEARNING

Introduction

In this chapter you will learn about:

- the teaching and learning environment;
- learning styles;
- key theories of learning;
- motivation and behaviour.

There are activities and examples to help you reflect on the above which will assist your understanding of some of the key theories of learning. At the end of each section is an extension activity to stretch and challenge your learning further.

This chapter contributes towards the following: scope (S), knowledge (K) and practice (P) aspects of the LLUK Professional Standards (A–F domains) for Teachers, Tutors and Trainers in the Lifelong Learning Sector:

ASI, AS2, AKI.I, AK2.I, AK2.2, AK4.I, API.I, AP2.2, AP3.I, AP4.I, AP6.2;
BSI, BKI.I, BKI.2, BKI.3, BK2.I, BK2.2, BK2.3, BPI.I, BPI.3;
CK3.I, CP3.I.

The teaching and learning environment

A suitable learning environment is crucial for effective learning to take place. This involves not only the venue and resources used, but also your attitude and the support you give to your learners. Learning can take place in a variety of contexts; for example, further education and sixth-form colleges, the workplace, adult and community learning centres, training organisations, the forces, public, private and voluntary sectors, prisons, industry and commerce. While learning can take place almost anywhere, not all environments will be totally suitable; however, it's how you teach your subject that will make learning effective.

You may be restricted by the availability of some rooms or resources; therefore you need to be imaginative with what you do have. Your learners don't need to know any problems your organisation has, as your professionalism should enable you to teach your subject effectively. However, you do need to take into account any health and safety issues and let your organisation know of any concerns. You need to establish a purposeful learning environment where you learners feel safe, secure, confident and valued. The venue, toilets and refreshment areas should be accessible and suitable to everyone. If your session includes a break, make sure you tell your learners what time this will be and for how long. If you don't, learners may not be concentrating on their learning but thinking about when they can go to the toilet or get a drink.

If you are teaching a practical subject, you will need a suitable environment so that you can demonstrate and your learners can practise. If you are teaching a theoretical subject, you may be fine in a classroom but you might need a computer, projector and interactive whiteboard. You might be delivering a seminar in a venue you have never visited before. If this is the case, it would be useful to telephone or visit in advance to check what facilities are available. Creating a good first impression, being organised and professional should help your learners feel they are in good hands.

Room layouts

The environment has three aspects: physical, social and learning. Each has an impact on the others and is equally important when planning your sessions. The physical environment is about the surroundings within which learning takes place; this need not be a traditional classroom but could be outdoors or another setting such as a community centre. The temperature, lighting and the area designated for learning can all affect the learning that takes place. You may need to close blinds to block out the sun, open a window to let in fresh air or even tidy rubbish away that has been left by the previous occupiers. The social environment is about how you put your learners at ease, establish a rapport with them and help them work together. The learning environment is concerned with giving your session a sense of purpose and direction by having clear aims, using suitable teaching and learning approaches, resources and assessment methods.

If you are teaching indoors, an important influence upon the way your session progresses and how you and your learners can communicate will be the room layout. You may not be able to control this if the furniture is in fixed positions. However, if you can, it is best to create an environment where learners can communicate with each other and see everything you are doing.

Desks in rows

This traditional classroom style does not lead to effective communication between learners. However, all learners can see the teacher as well as all presentation materials and resources being used. This layout is useful when delivering theoretical subjects if group work is not required. Learners tend to sit in the same seats at each session, the first ones in often head for the tables at the back. This layout without the tables would enable more chairs to be positioned in rows, allowing many learners to attend a session at the same time. This is known as lecture style. The teacher would need good voice projection to reach all learners at the back of the room, or use a microphone. The chairs might have a moveable arm on which to rest notes. If a learner is sitting in the middle of a row and needed to leave for any reason, they would disrupt the rest of the row of learners. (See Figure 2.1 on page 22.)

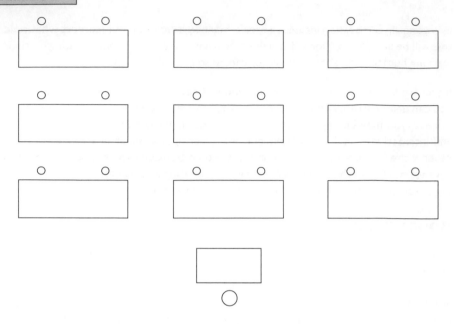

Figure 2.1 Desks in rows – classroom-style layout

Desks in groups

This 'cabaret' style is much better to allow learners to work together and interact during group activities. All learners can still see the teacher and any presentation materials being used. If room permits, tables could be moved so that they are not so close together, or placed at different angles. The teacher could sit beside the desk rather than behind so as not to create a barrier, or move around the room while teaching. See Figure 2.2 below.

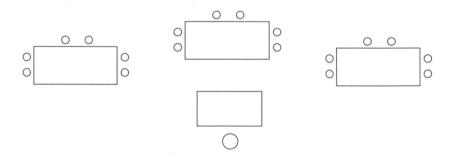

Figure 2.2 Cabaret-style layout

Horseshoe or 'u' shape

This style allows for large group discussions between the learners and the teacher, but is not good for small group work. Learners can still see the teacher and any presentation materials being used. Learners sitting at the very ends of tables may feel excluded from the group if activities are taking place. More tables could be added if necessary to close the gap and create an oblong shape, the teacher then becomes part of the group. See Figure 2.3 below.

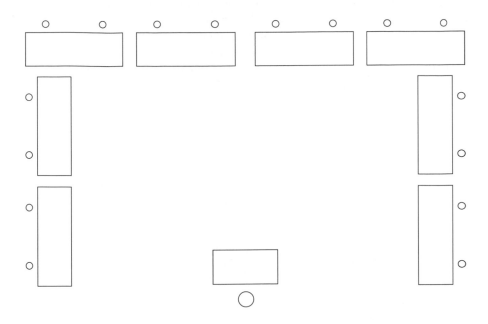

Figure 2.3 Horseshoe or U-shape layout

Boardroom style

This style allows for discussions and group work where a large table area is needed. If the teacher sits at the table with the learners, everyone can communicate and see each other. If the teacher sits separately, some learners will have their back to them and not be able to see a presentation screen if used. See Figure 2.4 below.

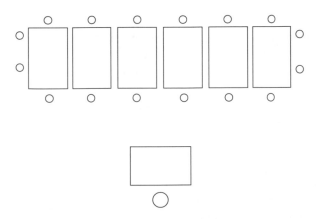

Figure 2.4 Boardroom-style layout

Other layouts

By experimenting with other layouts you can see how effective they are; for example, for individual, small group work and seminars. This can include the teacher as part of the group, with or without tables. Sometimes tables can create barriers between the teacher and the learners. If you need to move furniture, you should get another member of staff to help you beforehand and again afterwards. You will need to allow space for movement around the room and for bags and coats, to ensure there are no obstructions. Always return the room to its original layout at the end of your session. See Figure 2.5 below.

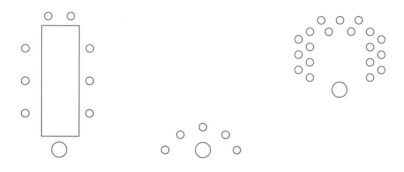

Figure 2.5 Other layouts

Activity

Think back to a really good, or a really bad experience you have had as a learner. Explain how the physical and social aspects had an impact upon your learning. Were there any other aspects that influenced your learning? What can you do to ensure your learners have a good experience with you?

You need to manage the learning environment to promote and encourage individual and group learning. The seating arrangements can have a big impact on learning. People like their comfort zones and you may find that learners will sit in the same place each time they are with you. This is often the place they sat at during the first session. This is useful to help you remember their names as you can sketch a seating plan and make a note of them. Remembering and using learner names will show respect, and encourage them to talk to you in confidence if they have any concerns. Moving learners around can either help or hinder their learning depending upon the group dynamics and learner maturity.

If possible, arrive early to set up the environment as you may find it hasn't been left in a suitable condition by the previous user.

Example

Harry arrived at 10.25 a.m. ready for his session which commenced at 10.30 a.m. He found the room was untidy with rubbish on the floor, three chairs were missing, writing was on the board and the computer wasn't connected to the projector. He became very flustered, his learners arrived while he was trying to prepare the room and he therefore didn't give a professional impression.

You need to ensure the physical environment is suitable not only for learning, but for social interaction too. Learning is more effective if it is in a suitable environment and you can meet all learning styles.

Health and safety considerations

Learners are entitled to learn in a safe and healthy environment. Under the Health and Safety at Work Act 1974 (HASAWA), health and safety is your responsibility as well as your organisation's. If you see a potential hazard, do something about it; don't wait for an accident to happen. Your learners may need to wear protective clothing or use hazardous substances for some activities; you will therefore need to find out what your organisation's procedures are for these. You might be using electrical equipment which will need regular checks by an appointed person in your organisation. You also need to make sure that any floor surfaces are not slippery, that any trailing wires are out of the way and any equipment your learners will be working with is safe and reliable. If you are teaching a subject that could be dangerous or hazardous, you may need to carry out risk assessments which should be documented. You could include your learners in this process to help them identify any issues or concerns, prior to their use.

You will need to know your organisation's accident and fire procedures such as the location of fire exits and meeting points, extinguishers and first aid facilities. You should inform your learners of these during their first session with you. If you have any learners who started late, you should always give them this information when they commence. You could include it in an induction handout or it may already be in a learner handbook they have been given. The Learning and Skills Council (now called the Skills Funding Agency) produced guidance for learners in the form of a handbook called *The Safe Learner (2007)*, which is a useful document to refer to when inducting your learners.

You should familiarise yourself with your organisation's health and safety policy and any other relevant legislation. You may have learners who have individual needs such as epilepsy or diabetes. It is important to know who they are, what you need to do, and who you need to contact in case of an emergency.

Extension Activity

Think about the subject you would like to teach and the environment you will teach in. Can you change anything to make the area more conducive to learning? What health and safety considerations might there be? Are there any restrictions regarding the resources your learners need to use; for example, cutting equipment? How can you involve your learners to identify and health and safety issues? Are there any records you need to complete beforehand or anyone you need to liaise with?

Learning styles

There is an old Chinese proverb: *I hear – I forget, I see – I remember, I do – I understand.* When you hear lots of information you may find it difficult to remember it all. If you can see something taking place that represents what you hear, you will hopefully remember more. However, if you actually carry out the task, you will understand the full process and remember how to do it again.

> *Studies show that over a period of three days, learning retention is as follows.*
> - *10% of what you read.*
> - *20% of what you hear.*
> - *30% of what you see.*
> - *50% of what you see and hear.*
> - *70% of what you say.*
> - *90% of what you say as you do.*
> (Pike, 1989)

Once learners put theory into practice they will begin to understand what they have learnt. Learners also have a particular learning style, a way that helps them to learn which is based on listening, seeing and doing. Your learners could take a short learning styles test prior to commencing your programme to identify what these are. However, what you may tend to do is teach your sessions in the style in which you learn best – although it will suit you, it may not suit your learners. Sue Crowley of the Institute for Learning (LSIS, 2009, page 8) stated:

> *Often new teachers teach as they were taught, then perhaps as they would like to have been taught, and finally they realise different people learn in different ways and a wider spectrum of teaching and learning approaches are needed and available.*

Fleming (2005)

Fleming stated that people can be grouped into four styles of learning: visual, aural, read/write and kinaesthetic (VARK).

Not all learners fall into one style; they may be multi-modal, i.e. a mixture of two or more styles enabling learning to take place more quickly.

Visual

Visual (seeing) learners usually:

- are meticulous and neat in appearance;
- find verbal instructions difficult;
- memorise by looking at pictures;
- notice details;
- observe rather than act or talk;
- like watching videos/DVDs.

Aural

Aural (listening and talking) learners usually:

- are easily distracted;
- enjoy talking and listening to others;
- have difficulty with written instructions;
- hum, sing and whisper or talk out loud;
- ask questions;
- don't like noisy environments.

Read/write

Read/write (reading and writing) learners usually:

- are good spellers and have good handwriting;
- enjoy research;
- like rewriting what others have written;
- like to read books;
- use a dictionary and thesaurus;
- write lists and make notes.

Kinaesthetic

Kinaesthetic (doing) learners usually:

- are tactile towards others;
- do not like reading and are often poor spellers;
- enjoy worksheets and discussions;
- fidget with pens while studying;
- like practical activities;
- use their hands while talking.

Honey and Mumford (1992)

Honey and Mumford suggest learners are a mixture of the four styles:

- activist;

- pragmatist;

- theorist;

- reflector.

Activist

Activist learners like to deal with new problems and experiences and like lots of activities to keep them busy. They love challenges and are enthusiastic.

Pragmatist

Pragmatist learners like to apply what they have learned to practical situations. They like logical reasons for doing something.

Theorist

Theorist learners need time to take in information, they prefer to read lots of material and think about something before applying it.

Reflector

Reflector learners think deeply about what they are learning and the activities they could do to apply this learning. They like things that have been tried and tested.

Activity

Consider something you have recently learnt; for example, using a new mobile phone. Did you: jump right in and press all the buttons (activist); look briefly at the instructions and then have a go (pragmatist); read the instructions thoroughly, then carry them out (theorist); or become confident at using the phone for calls and texts before considering its other uses (reflector)?

It is always useful to get your learners to carry out a learning styles test. It can be fun and lead to an interesting discussion, as well as helping you plan your teaching and learning approaches to reach their learning styles. It also empowers learners to adapt information in a way that they are comfortable with, for example, using a voice recorder rather than handwriting notes.

If you have access to the internet, log on to the website www.vark-learn.com and carry out the learning styles test. It only takes a few minutes and you will receive an instant result. Locate another suitable learning styles questionnaire and carry it out. Compare and contrast your results. Decide which test could be used with your own learners and how you could make use of the results to help their learning. If you don't have internet access, research different learning styles in relevant textbooks.

Key theories of learning

Learners need to know why it is important for them to learn, what they are going to learn and how they will do this. Setting clear aims of what you want your learners to achieve is the starting point; summarising regularly, varying your teaching approaches and taking learning styles into account will all help. Having a sense of humour and making learning interesting and fun will help your learners remember key points. Your learners need to believe that what they are learning has real value and meaning. You also need to treat each learner as an individual and with respect, using their name wherever possible. You should always introduce yourself to your learners; you could keep your name visible somewhere or wear a name badge. This should encourage them to approach you or ask questions.

There are lots of theories regarding how people learn. These theories will have been based on ideas, thoughts and experiences. Some are quite old, but are tried and trusted; others are fairly recent. You may even come up with your own theory or challenge existing ones. All people learn differently, perhaps influenced by experiences in their childhood, school, personal or professional relationships. When you learn something new, you will probably adapt, change or modify your behaviour as a result, and the same will apply to your learners. This section will briefly explain some of these theories, which you may wish to research further.

Sensory theory

Laird (1985) stated that learning occurs when the five senses of sight, hearing, touch, smell and taste are stimulated. Laird's theory suggests that if multi-senses are stimulated, greater learning takes place. You could therefore adapt your teaching styles and resources to enable your learners to use as many of their senses as possible.

When you were a child, if you saw something that interested you, you would touch it, probably putting it in your mouth if it was small, shaking it to hear if it made a noise and putting it near your nose to smell it. You would soon learn if something tasted nasty not to put it in your mouth again. Therefore, a change in your behaviour took place as a result.

Conditions of learning

Gagne (1985) stated that there are several different types or levels of learning. Each different type requires different types of teaching. Gagne identified five major conditions of learning. These are:

- verbal information;
- intellectual skills;
- cognitive strategies;
- motor skills;
- attitudes.

Different internal and external conditions are required for each category of learning. For example, for motor skills to be learnt, there must be the opportunity for your learner to practise new skills rather than just learn about them. For attitudes, your learner must be able to explore these; for example, discussing environmental issues. In addition, this theory outlines nine events that activate the processes needed for effective learning to take place. Gagne believed all teaching and learning sessions should include this sequence of events. Each has a corresponding cognitive process (in brackets below).

1. Gaining attention (reception).
2. Informing learners of the objective (expectancy).
3. Stimulating recall of prior learning (retrieval).
4. Presenting the stimulus (selective perception).
5. Providing learning guidance (semantic encoding).
6. Eliciting performance (responding).
7. Providing feedback (reinforcement).
8. Assessing performance (retrieval).
9. Enhancing retention and transfer (generalisation).

Example

Sue can ensure all these events take place in her sessions by:

1. *Gaining attention – showing an example of what the learners will achieve during the session, e.g. an iced wedding cake.*
2. *Identifying the objective – stating that the learners will be able to ice a wedding cake by the end of the session.*
3. *Recalling prior learning – asking the learners if they have ever iced a wedding cake before.*
4. *Presenting stimulus – explaining how they will ice the wedding cake and what they will need to use.*

Example (continued)

5. *Guiding learning – demonstrating how to ice a wedding cake.*
6. *Eliciting performance – encouraging the learners to begin icing a wedding cake.*
7. *Providing feedback – informing the learners how they are progressing.*
8. *Assessing performance – ensuring the learners are correctly icing the wedding cake by observing and asking questions.*
9. *Enhancing retention/transfer – summarising the learning relating it to real life events and explaining what will be covered in the next session.*

Experiential theory

Kolb (1984) proposed a four-stage experiential learning cycle by which people understand their experiences, and as a result, modify their behaviour. It is based on the idea that the more often a learner reflects on a task, the more often they have the opportunity to modify and refine their efforts. See Figure 2.6 below.

Figure 2.6 Kolb's (1984) experiential learning cycle

Concrete experience is about experiencing or immersing yourself in the task and is the first stage in which a person simply carries out the task assigned. This is the *doing* stage.

Observation and reflection involve stepping back from the task and reviewing what has been done and experienced. Your values, attitudes and beliefs can influence your thinking at this stage. This is the stage of *thinking* about what you have done.

Abstract conceptualisation involves interpreting the events that have been carried out and making sense of them. This is the stage of *planning* how you will do it differently.

Active experimentation enables you to take the new learning and predict what is likely to happen next or what actions should be taken to refine the way the task is done again. This is the *redoing* stage based upon experience and reflection.

The process of learning can begin at any stage and is continuous, i.e. there is no limit to the number of cycles you can make in a learning situation. This theory suggests that without reflection, people would continue to repeat their mistakes.

Example

Wang is taking an accounting programme which has an examination at the end. If he fails he will not know why he has failed. He will need to wait another three months before he can retake the examination. During the programme, he could experience the learning process, but not reflect upon what he might be doing wrong that may lead to him failing the examination. He therefore could not modify his behaviour and try again. If he took a programme with ongoing assessment instead of an examination at the end, he would have the opportunity to go through the full cycle. He would have the experience, reflect upon it due to ongoing feedback, think how he could improve and then experiment to try again.

You are probably familiar with the saying *you learn by experience*. You might find that doing a task, then thinking about it, leads you to plan how you would do it differently next time. Repeating tasks will help your learners learn, whether this is a practical task or a theoretical subject.

Humanist theory

Rogers (1983) and others developed the theory of facilitative learning. This is based upon a belief that people have a natural eagerness to learn and that learning involves changing your own concept of yourself. This theory suggests that learning will take place if the person delivering it acts as a facilitator. They should establish an atmosphere in which their learners feel comfortable and able to discuss new ideas, if they are not threatened by external factors.

Example

Vicky is due to teach a Digital Photography for Beginners evening class. There is no syllabus, therefore she has planned what she thinks is relevant, based on the last time she taught it. However, she remembered being told by an observer in her class last term that she should consider the needs of her learners more. Therefore, at the first session, she has decided to encourage her learners to tell her if they have anything they would like to learn, which she hadn't planned to teach. This will enable her to facilitate her sessions to cover their expectations and help make her learners feel comfortable to discuss the topics.

Behaviourist theory

Skinner (1974) believed that behaviour is a function of its consequences. Your learner will repeat the desired behaviour if positive reinforcement follows. If negative feedback is given, the behaviour should not be repeated. Giving immediate feedback, whether positive or negative, should enable your learner to behave in a certain way.

Positive reinforcement or rewards can include verbal feedback such as *That's great, you've produced that document without any errors* or *You're certainly getting on well with that task* through to more tangible rewards such as a certificate at the end of the programme or a promotion at work.

Example

Jamie was sawing a piece of wood and hadn't paid attention to the health and safety regulations. The saw kept slipping and he cut his hand. His teacher gave him negative feedback and this, along with his cut, ensured he was more careful in future.

The Peter principle

Peter and Hull (1969) stated that people are promoted to their highest level of competence, after which further promotion raises them to a level just beyond this and they become incompetent. These levels are as follows.

- Unconscious incompetence – you don't know how to do something, but don't know that you don't know this. To reach the next level, you need to know what it is that you don't know.

- Conscious incompetence – you know what you want to do, and start to appreciate the gap in your competence. To reach the next level you need to know how to become competent.

- Conscious competence – you can do what you set out to do, but have to give it a lot of attention. Through repeated practice you can reach the next level.

- Unconscious competence – you can perform a skill easily without giving it a great deal of thought. Once you achieve unconscious competence, you are at a level which suits your ability at the time. However, if you are promoted or try something different, you may return to the first level and become unconsciously incompetent again.

This is useful to know, as your learners may reach and stay at one of these levels.

Renuka has just started a Using Spreadsheets programme, having previously only used a computer for e-mails. She doesn't yet know how to use a spreadsheet or the functions it can perform – she is at the unconscious incompetence level. After learning how to set up a spreadsheet, she now wishes to perform some calculations; she knows she wants to do this but doesn't know how. This is the conscious incompetence level. Renuka soon learns how to perform calculations and practises this at the conscious competence level. She isn't quite at the unconscious competence level yet, where she could do it without thinking.

Domains of learning

Bloom (1956) stated that learning often goes through the following stages which should lead to a change in behaviour. These stages are:

- attention;

- perception;

- understanding;

- short-/long-term memory;

- change in behaviour.

These stages can affect your learners' thinking, emotions and actions, and Bloom called them domains: cognitive, affective and psycho-motor (respectively). Think of cognitive as the head (thinking), affective as the heart (emotions) and psycho-motor as the hands (actions).

When teaching your subject, you need to consider which domain you want to reach, for example:

- cognitive (subject – geography) learners will state the reasons for coastal erosion;

- affective (subject – the environment) learners will discuss their ideas for recycling;

- psycho-motor (subject – bricklaying) learners will build a two-foot high wall.

You will also need to consider how you can address all learning styles, particularly if your subject is psycho-motor and the majority of your learners are read/write.

Compare and contrast two or more of the learning theories in this section. How will they affect the way you teach and the way your learners will learn? Research other learning theories such as those which come under the headings of pragmatists and constructivists.

Motivation and behaviour

You need to be aware of what motivates your learners, as their keenness to learn will affect their behaviour during your sessions. A learner attending a session because they have been told to may not be as motivated as a learner who is there for personal fulfilment.

Motivation

Motivation is either intrinsic (from within), meaning the learner wants to learn for their own fulfilment, or extrinsic (from without), meaning there may be an external factor motivating the learner; for example, a promotion at work.

Whatever level of motivation your learners have will be transformed, for better or worse, by what happens during their learning experience with you. You therefore need to promote a professional relationship that leads to individual learning and trust. Some learners may seem naturally enthusiastic about learning, but many need or expect you to inspire, challenge, engage and stimulate them.

Many factors affect a learner's motivation to work and to learn; for example, interest in the subject matter, perception of its usefulness, a general desire to achieve, self-confidence and self-esteem, as well as patience and persistence. Not all learners are motivated by the same values, needs, desires, or wants. Some of your learners will be motivated by the approval of others, some by overcoming personal challenges.

To help motivate your learners you can:

- ask open questions, not closed questions, which just lead to yes or no responses;
- avoid creating intense competition, although some competition can be challenging and fun;
- be aware of their attention-span limits;
- challenge and support those who need it;
- give ongoing constructive feedback;
- maintain an organised and orderly atmosphere;
- make tasks interesting, practical and relevant;
- negotiate clear targets;
- treat them with respect and as individuals;
- vary your teaching approaches to reach all learning styles;
- give praise and encouragement.

Maslow (1987) introduced a *Hierarchy of Needs* in 1954 after rejecting the idea that human behaviour was determined by childhood events. He felt that obstacles should be removed that prevent a person from achieving their goals. He argued there are five needs which represent different levels of motivation which must be met. The highest level was labelled self-actualisation, meaning people are fully functional, possess a healthy personality, and take responsibility for themselves and their actions. He also believed that people should be able to move through these needs to the highest level provided they are given an education that promotes growth.

Figure 2.7 below shows the needs expressed as they might relate to learning, starting at the base of the pyramid.

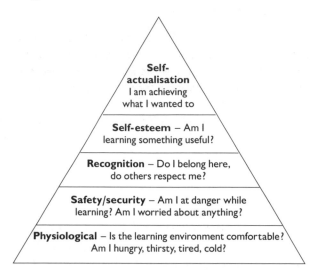

Figure 2.7 Maslow's (1987) Hierarchy of needs expressed in educational terms

When learners satisfy their needs at one level, they should be able to progress to the next. Something may set them back a level, but they will keep striving upwards. It is these needs that motivate learning to take place. However, some people may not want to progress through the levels, and may be quite content where they are at that moment in their life.

To help your learners' motivation, always ensure that the learning environment you create meets your learners' first-level needs. This will enable them to feel comfortable and secure enough to learn and progress to the higher levels. You will need to appreciate that some learners may not have these lower needs met in their home lives, making it difficult for them to move on to the higher levels.

Always try to establish a purposeful learning environment where your learners can feel safe, secure, confident and valued.

Example

Ruth was due to teach a session from 5 p.m. to 7 p.m. She arrived early and noticed the room was hot and stuffy so opened the windows. She also realised that most of her learners might not have had a chance to eat something prior to the session. When they arrived she told them they could have an early break to enable them to get refreshments. After break, she kept one window open to keep some fresh air in the room and also allowed her learners to have bottled water if they wished. This ensured her learners' first-level needs were met.

While you may be very good at teaching your subject, you might have no control over the environment and will need to create a suitable atmosphere. Your enthusiasm and passion for your subject will help engage your learners. If you can also make your session interesting and varied, your learners will enjoy the experience and remember more about the subject and you, rather than the environment or lack of facilities.

Behaviour and disruption

To get through a session without any disruptions would be wonderful, but this very rarely happens. You might have a learner who arrives late, an inquisitive learner who always wants to know more, or just someone asking to leave the room to get a drink of water. Whatever the disruption may be, you need to handle this professionally to minimise any effect it may have on teaching and learning. Don't just ignore the behaviour, address it immediately. However, with experience you will realise that some things can be ignored providing this does not affect the safety of your learners.

Example

Philip was giving a presentation to a group of 15 learners during an afternoon session. Three learners in the group began talking among themselves about what they did at the weekend. Rather than reprimand them, Philip decided to stop speaking altogether and use eye contact with them. They soon realised he was no longer speaking but looking at them. Because he was silent, they stopped talking and paid attention again.

Usually, disruptions or changes in behaviour occur because a learner doesn't follow the ground rules; for example, their mobile phone rings or they do something other than that which you have asked them to do. If this is the case, politely ask them to stop, remind them of the ground rules and how they are also disrupting their peers' learning. Other occurrences happen because people are bored, they don't understand what you are saying, their attention span is different, or you are not challenging them enough. You could give an alternative activity to stretch and challenge learning, get them involved with other learners or have a quick one-to-one chat to find out why they are behaving that way.

You may find it useful to maintain a record of the behaviour of your learners during your sessions to help you prepare for future incidents. For example, do some learners become disruptive after a certain time period has elapsed; when seated in particular combinations with others, when asked to carry out a theory task, or when practical activities are taking place? This information can be useful when planning future sessions; for example, the timing of breaks, the use of energiser activities or planning group work. Behaviour patterns could highlight the need for additional support as disruption could be a way of asking for help. You should lead by example and always be polite, show respect and say *please* and *thank you* to help encourage this behaviour in your learners.

Your learners may not be attending voluntarily, or they may be there for social reasons rather than having an interest in achieving a qualification. They may therefore not be as keen as you would like them to be and you will need to keep them continuously interested and motivated.

You can help maintain motivation and good behaviour by including all learners during discussions and activities, keeping your sessions active wherever possible and teaching your subject in an interesting and challenging way. Ultimately, you need to find your own way of dealing with situations based upon your experiences. Don't show favouritism, lose your temper, make threats or touch learners inappropriately. Try to have a positive approach, praise performance and good behaviour and be consistent and fair to everyone. Most learners respond positively to a well-organised programme taught by an enthusiastic teacher who has a genuine interest in them and the subject.

Extension Activity

Research other motivation theorists such as Elton Mayo (1880–1949) Hawthorne Effect theory, Frederick Herzberg (1923–2000) Two factor theory and Douglas McGregor (1906–1964) X and Y theory. Compare and contrast these. How will their theories affect the way you motivate your learners? What are your own theories of motivation?

Summary

In this chapter you have learnt about:

- the teaching and learning environment;
- learning styles;
- key theories of learning;
- motivation and behaviour.

Theory focus

References and further information

Bloom, BS (1956) *Taxonomy of Educational Objectives: The Classification of educational goals*. New York: McKay.

Fleming, N (2005) *Teaching and Learning Styles: VARK strategies*. Honolulu: Honolulu Community College.

Gagne, R (1985) *The Conditions of Learning* (4th edn). New York: Holt, Rinehart & Winston.

Honey, P and Mumford, A (1992) *The Manual of Learning Styles* (3rd edn). Maidenhead: Peter Honey Associates.

Kolb, DA (1984) *Experiential Learning: Experience as the Source of Learning and Development*. New Jersey: Prentice-Hall.

Laird, D (1985) *Approaches to Training and Development*. Harlow: Addison Wesley.

Learning and Skills Council (2007) *Learner Health, Safety and Welfare: The safe learner blueprint*. Coventry: LSC.

LSIS (2009) *Centres for Excellence in Teacher Training: CETT Standard*. Learning and Skills Improvement Service Newsletter issue I.

Maslow, AH (1987) (edited by Frager, R) *Motivation and Personality* (3rd revised edn). New York: Pearson Education Ltd.

Peter, LJ and Hull, R (1969) *The Peter Principle: Why things always go wrong*. New York: William Morrow and Company.

Pike, RW (1989) *Creative Training Techniques Handbook*. Minneapolis MN: Lakewood Books.

Rogers, CR (1983) *Freedom to Learn for the 80s*. Columbus, OH: Merrill.

Skinner, BF (1974) *About Behaviorism*. San Francisco, CA: Knopf.

Wallace, S (2007) *Managing Behaviour in the Lifelong Learning Sector* (2nd edn). Exeter: Learning Matters.

Websites

Cognitive learningstyles – http://tip.psychology.org/styles.html

Health and Safety Executive – www.hse.gov.uk

Informal Education Encyclopedia – www.infed.org/encyclopaedia.htm

Learning styles test – www.vark-learn.com

Learning theories – www.learning-theories.com

Pragmatists and constructivists – http://classweb.gmu.edu/ndabbagh/Resources/IDKB/models_theories.htm

Introduction

In this chapter you will learn about:

- identifying needs of the organisation, teachers and learners;
- initial assessment;
- potential needs of learners and points of referral;
- equality and diversity;
- promoting inclusion.

There are activities and examples to help you reflect on the above which will assist your understanding of how to identify the needs of the organisation, teachers and learners. There are extension activities to stretch and challenge your learning further.

This chapter contributes towards the following: scope (S), knowledge (K) and practice (P) aspects of the LLUK Professional Standards (A–F domains) for Teachers, Tutors and Trainers in the Lifelong Learning Sector:

ASI, AS2, AS3, AS5, AS6, AS7, AKI.I, AK2.I, AK3.I, AK5.2, API.I, AP2.I, AP2.2, AP3.I, AP5.I, AP5.2, AP6.2;
BSI, BS3, BS4, BK2.5, BK3.4, BK3.5, BK4.I, BP2.5, BP3.5, BP4.I;
CK3.2, CK3.5, CP3.2, CP3.3, CP4.2;
DSI, DS2, DK2.2, DK2.2, DPI.I;
ESI, ES3, EKI.I, EK2.I;
FSI, FS2, FS4, FKI.I, FKI.2, FK2.I, FK4.I, FK4.2, FPI.I, FPI.2, FP2.I, FP3.I, FP4.I, FP4.2.

Identifying needs of the organisation, teachers and learners

Identifying and understanding the needs of all parties involved in the teaching and learning process will help ensure your practice is effective.

Organisational needs

The starting point for planning teaching and learning is usually based upon the needs of your organisation; for example, the curriculum which is to be offered. The qualifications and programmes which make up the curriculum will be decided by local needs; for example, business and employment. Other considerations may include funding from external agencies, as some programmes are offered only if financial support can be obtained. External agencies such as awarding organisations will give approval for accredited qualifications to be delivered at your organisation. They will produce a syllabus or qualification handbook for each subject which gives details of what must be taught and assessed. If learners successfully achieve the requirements, they will receive a certificate endorsed by the awarding organisation. Your organisation will recruit relevant experienced staff to meet their curriculum needs.

If there is a demand, *bespoke* programmes could be created to meet a particular need and be offered in house; for example, at a place of employment. These are known as *non-accredited* programmes and your organisation may issue certificates of attendance. These will prove a person was there, but not that they necessarily learnt anything. Assessment would need to take place to determine what that person actually learnt, enabling a certificate of competence to be issued. These types of programme are often classed as *full cost* and are paid for by the employer or the learner.

Programmes and qualifications can be short-, medium- or long-term and may be offered at various times of the day or evening, at various locations, depending upon needs. Different models of delivery can be used such as formal attendance, open, online, distance learning, flexible, or blended learning which combines technology with learning.

If the programme you teach is advertised on your organisation's website, in a prospectus, leaflets or in the local press, make sure you read it to check it is correct. If what you plan to teach is different from that advertised, there will be confusion when your learners commence.

Different models of delivery will influence what you must and could teach to your learners. The *product* model focuses upon the outcomes of a programme; for example, what learners need to know to pass an examination, test or assignment. The teacher often just teaches what must be taught to get the learner through. What could be taught isn't taken into consideration, often due to time constraints, and doesn't benefit the learner in the long term.

Example

Samantha is taking GCSE French and just wants to pass the qualification. Her teacher covers only what is in the syllabus (what must *be taught) and does not cover anything else which could help Samantha if she visits France in the future.*

The *process* model focuses on the content of the programme and other relevant knowledge and skills that could be learnt and applied.

Example

Kelly is taking a word-processing qualification. She is paying for the programme herself and is prepared to continue until she feels competent. As she has never used a computer before, she has asked her teacher to help her learn keyboard skills and file-management skills. These are in addition to word-processing skills. She is therefore getting the benefit of what could be taught as well as what must be.

When planning what to teach, you will need to use the syllabus as your starting point, ensuring you teach all the required content. Additional aspects that could be taught to add value to the content will be based upon how much time you have and the needs of your organisation and learners.

Teacher needs

All teachers should be knowledgeable and current not only in their subject knowledge but they should also know how to use innovative ways to teach their subject. Your needs as a teacher might include updating your subject knowledge, working towards teaching qualifications and/or learning new skills. This will all count towards your continuing professional development (CPD) which is a requirement of the Institute for Learning (IfL).

> CPD gives the public, learners, the teaching community and the sector confidence that teachers, trainers, tutors and assessors are continuously improving their skills, knowledge and expertise. CPD is the hallmark of the professional.
>
> (Institute for Learning, 2009)

You need a suitable environment in which to teach your subject. You may not be able to change the setting; however, you could make it more stimulating by displaying posters or changing the layout of the furniture (if possible). You will also need various resources to teach your subject effectively; for example, computers, models, books, etc. Whether you can have these might depend upon the finances available. If your organisation can't afford to buy up-to-date textbooks you could place the onus upon your learners to purchase them or access them from the local library.

There are certain things you must know; for example, what and who you will be teaching, for how long, where and when. Knowing this will help you plan your sessions effectively. You will also need to know the people at your organisation who can support you; for example, administration staff and caretakers. When you start teaching, you should have a mentor, someone in the same subject area as yourself. They should show you around the premises, introduce you to relevant staff members and give you advice and support as necessary.

You might find it useful to create a toolkit of items you will regularly use when teaching. This could contain pens, board markers, a wireless remote control for electronic presentations, paper, a small clock, stapler, hole punch and other relevant items. It's useful to have a few extra pre-prepared activities or quizzes that you could use if you have spare time at the end of sessions, or if some learners finish an activity earlier than others.

Learner needs

Identifying your learners' needs can take place as part of the application process, during an interview or when they commence the programme. Information, advice and guidance (IAG) should be given to learners regarding their programme choice and this should be clear, unambiguous and impartial to ensure it meets their needs and capability. Identifying any individual learner needs prior to commencement will help you plan your teaching to meet these. However, depending upon the type of programme you are teaching, you might not always be able to do this in advance. As a result, some learners may take a programme which is unsuitable for them. If possible, try to have contact with all learners before they are committed to taking a particular qualification.

Some learners may be embarrassed or not wish to divulge personal information on application forms or at an interview. You could have an informal chat with them to find out if they have any needs or specific requirements; for example, dyslexia or dyscalculia. If you are unsure about how to help your learners, just ask, as they are best placed to know how you could support them.

You should discuss the requirements of the qualification with your learners, along with the range of services and agencies that are available to assist with any specific needs. Impartial advice should also be available regarding career progression, job search, preparation for interviews and more. Your learners will benefit greatly from this service and will be more likely to finish the programme and successfully achieve their qualification.

Activity

Find out what the information, advice and guidance (IAG) procedures are at your organisation. How will you be involved with this process and how will it benefit your learners? If you are not yet teaching, how do you think IAG staff can support learners effectively?

Initial assessment

This is the formal way of ascertaining your learners' prior skills and/or knowledge of the subject to be taken and whether they have any specific needs to help them meet the qualification requirements. It should be carried out prior to, or at the beginning of the programme. There could be particular entry requirements for your subject and an initial assessment or interview would ascertain if these had been met. Diagnostic assessments can be used to evaluate a learner's skills, knowledge, strengths and areas for development in a particular area. It could be that your learner feels they are capable of achieving at a higher level than the initial assessments determine. The results will give a thorough indication of not only the level at which your learner needs to be placed for their subject but also which specific aspects they need to improve on. Diagnostic tests can also be used to ascertain information regarding literacy, numeracy and computer skills. Information gained from these tests will help you plan your sessions to meet any individual needs and/or to arrange further training and support if necessary. You should not take learners just because you need the numbers to make a group, as the programme may not be suitable for them and they may leave.

Using initial assessments will help you to identify any particular aspects which may otherwise go unnoticed and ensure you are meeting equality and diversity require-ments.

Identifying learning styles will help you decide the teaching and learning approaches to use (see Chapter 2).

Initial assessment will:

- allow for differentiation and individual requirements to be met;
- ensure learners are on the right programme at the right level;
- ensure the learner knows what is expected of them;
- identify an appropriate pace at which each learner will progress;
- identify an appropriate starting point for each learner;
- identify any information which needs to be shared with colleagues;
- identify any specific additional support needs;
- identify learning styles;
- identify previous experience, achievements and transferable skills;
- identify specific requirements; for example, literacy, numeracy and computer skills;
- inspire and motivate learners;
- involve learners, giving them confidence to negotiate suitable targets.

The results of initial assessments should help you negotiate individual learning plans (ILPs) or action plans with your learners, ensuring they are on the right programme at the right level.

Extension Activity

Find out what initial and diagnostic assessments are used at your organisation. Will it be your responsibility to administer these, or is there a specialist person to do this? How will you use the results? If you are not yet teaching, research suitable ones that you could use with your learners in future.

Potential needs of learners and points of referral

Some learners will have needs, barriers or challenges to learning that may affect their attendance and/or achievement. Hopefully you can ascertain these prior to your learners commencing. However, others may occur during the programme and you would need to plan a suitable course of action to help the learners, or refer them to an appropriate specialist or agency.

Behaviour Code 3 of the IfL Code of Professional Practice states:

> *Members shall take reasonable care to ensure the safety and welfare of learners and comply with relevant statutory provisions to support their wellbeing and development.*

(IfL, 2008)

If you can be proactive and notice potential needs before they become issues, you might be able to alleviate your learners' concerns. Otherwise, you will need to be reactive to the issue and deal with it professionally and sensitively. Your learners may trust you and tell you something confidential; however, you may need to pass this information on to more experienced people, particularly if your learner is vulnerable and/or in need of expert help. See Table 3.1 below.

Table 3.1 Examples of potential needs, barriers and challenges

<ul><li>abilities;</li><li>access to or fear of technology;</li><li>age;</li><li>behavioural difficulties;</li><li>bullying in person and cyber-bullying;</li><li>childcare arrangements;</li><li>culture and language differences;</li><li>disabilities;</li><li>discipline;</li><li>dyslexia, dyscalculia, dyspraxia, etc.;</li><li>emotional or psychological problems;</li><li>environment;</li><li>faith and religion;</li><li>family commitments;</li><li>fears; for example, technology, change, not knowing anyone else, previous school experiences;</li><li>finance;</li><li>hearing or visual impairment;</li><li>housing problems;</li><li>hyperactivity;</li></ul>	<ul><li>lack of confidence, motivation, social skills;</li><li>lack of resources;</li><li>lack of support;</li><li>language;</li><li>learning difficulties and disabilities;</li><li>limited basic skills such as literacy, numeracy and ICT;</li><li>mental health issues;</li><li>mixed-ability learning styles;</li><li>mobility problems;</li><li>past experiences;</li><li>peer pressure;</li><li>personal/work/home circumstances;</li><li>physical, medical, mental or health conditions;</li><li>poor attendance;</li><li>previous learning experiences;</li><li>social problems;</li><li>status of the group;</li><li>timing issues;</li><li>transport problems;</li><li>weather.</li></ul>

Points of referral

You may encounter learners with varying degrees of needs; therefore you should remain impartial, but sensitive. You may feel you can deal with some of these yourself; however, it's best to seek advice or refer your learner to someone who can help. If a learner discloses something which is covered by the Disability Discrimination Act (DDA) Part Four (1995 amended 2005), the whole organisation is deemed to know. It is therefore important that any issues are communicated to all concerned, and acted upon.

Example

Dave informed his teacher that he is dyslexic and asked if any handouts could be printed on cream paper. He also asked if anyone minded if he used a digital recorder during the sessions, as he preferred to listen to this afterwards rather than make notes. His teacher asked the group if they were all happy to have handouts on cream paper and whether they minded Dave recording the session. All the group agreed to his requests. The teacher also informed a colleague who taught Dave to ensure they were being consistent with their support.

You should always refer your learners to an appropriate specialist or agency if you can't deal with their needs. Never feel you have to solve any learner problems yourself and don't get personally involved. You will need to find out what is available internally within your organisation or where you could refer them externally. See Table 3.2 below.

Table 3.2 Example points of referral

Internal	External
<ul><li>accommodation officers;</li><li>careers advisers;</li><li>colleagues;</li><li>counsellors;</li><li>examination officers;</li><li>financial services staff;</li><li>first-aiders;</li><li>health and welfare officers;</li><li>information, advice and guidance staff;</li><li>interpreters;</li><li>learning support staff;</li><li>mentors;</li><li>student union representatives;</li><li>teachers.</li></ul>	<ul><li>awarding organisations;</li><li>banks or building societies;</li><li>carers;</li><li>charities;</li><li>childcare agencies;</li><li>Citizen's Advice Bureau;</li><li>employers;</li><li>health centres and general practitioners;</li><li>Job Centre Plus;</li><li>motoring and transport organisations;</li><li>police;</li><li>Samaritans;</li><li>telephone helplines and agencies such as abuse, alcohol, Childline, Crimestoppers, debt, drug, lesbian and gay switchboard, gambling, NHS Direct, parentline, victim support;</li><li>websites which are relevant.</li></ul>

Activity

What potential needs, barriers or challenges do you feel learners might have? If you are currently teaching, find out what relevant points of referral are available to meet these needs, and review how effective they might be.

Equality and diversity

Equality is about the rights of learners to have access to, attend, and participate in their chosen learning experience. This should be regardless of age, ability and/or circumstances. Any inequality and discrimination should be tackled to ensure fairness, decency and respect among your learners. Equal opportunity is a concept underpinned by legislation to provide relevant and appropriate access for the participation, development and advancement of all individuals and groups. In the past, equality has often been described as *everyone being the same* or *having the same opportunities*. Nowadays, it can be described as *everyone being different, but having equal rights*.

Diversity is about valuing and respecting the differences in learners, regardless of age, ability and/or circumstances, or any other individual characteristics they may have. If you have two or more learners, you will experience diversity. You may have a mixed group of learners with different levels of experience who are aiming to achieve the same qualification but at a different level. You could therefore set different activities and targets for the different assessment criteria of the qualification.

When teaching, you should always ensure you:

- are non-judgemental;
- challenge any direct or indirect discrimination, stereotyping, prejudice, harassment, bullying and biased attitudes by yourself or other learners;
- challenge your own values, attitudes and beliefs so that you are not imposing these upon your learners;
- do not have favourite learners or give some more attention than others;
- do not indulge the minority at the expense of the majority;
- ensure particular groups are not offended; for example, faiths or religions;
- ensure particular learners are not disadvantaged or overly advantaged;
- treat all learners with respect and dignity;
- use activities and assessments which are pitched at the right level;
- use questions which are worded so as not to cause embarrassment to learners.

Incorporating activities based around equality and diversity and the local community and society within which your learners live and work could help your learners be more understanding and tolerant of each other. You also need to prepare them for the world outside their own living and working environment in case they move else-where in the future.

To ensure you comply with the Equality Act 2006, you need to be proactive in all aspects of equality and diversity, and make sure your teaching style and resources promote and include all learners in respect of the six strands:

- age;

- disability;

- gender;

- race;

- religion and belief;

- sexual orientation.

The Act was further enhanced in 2010 to bring disability, sex, race and other grounds of discrimination within one piece of legislation. You could create activities to carry out with your learners such as discussions or quizzes to help raise awareness, perhaps during the induction process or group tutorials. Wherever possible, try to use naturally occurring opportunities.

Example

Mary was teaching a catering programme to a mixed group of learners from various backgrounds and faiths. As Chinese New Year was approaching she decided to use it as a theme and create different menus around it. This opened up a discussion about the Chinese culture, which the group found interesting and meaningful. She decided she would research other cultures, faiths and religions to incorporate them during their sessions.

Other opportunities could include discussing events in the news such as racist attacks, or an issue in a particular television programme such as disability or ageism. Try to encourage learners not to make assumptions; for example, *foreigners always take the jobs of British people*, or *mothers always take time off work to look after their children*. If conversations like these occur, take the opportunity to challenge them.

Extension Activity

What issues regarding equality and diversity do you feel you may encounter with your learners, and how will you deal with these? How can you embed aspects of equality and diversity within your sessions?

Promoting inclusion

Inclusion is about involving all your learners, treating them equally and fairly, without directly or indirectly excluding anyone. Some learners could feel excluded during your session if their particular needs were not met. You therefore need to know in advance, through initial assessment or the induction process, just what these needs are. Inclusion is also about attitudes as well as behaviour, as learners can be affected by the words or actions of others. You are not teaching your subject to a group of learners who are all the same, but to a group of individuals with different experiences, abilities and needs which should be recognised and respected. Try to promote a positive culture of equality of opportunity within your sessions whereby all learners can attend, participate and feel safe and valued.

Example

Tariq has a group of 16 learners of different levels of experience and ability. He ensures each of his sessions includes a group activity where the full group is split into smaller groups of four learners who will research and present a topic. Tariq ensures each group is made up of different learners each time which enables all learners to get to know and work with each other, and share experiences. He gives each group member responsibility for an aspect of the activity which ensures all members of the group must work together to achieve the task. This way, all his learners are included in the activity and play an active part.

Using your learners' names when talking to them, using eye contact and speaking personally to them during each session will help ensure they feel included. See Table 3.3 page 50.

If you can develop the conditions for learning that are based on respect and trust and address the needs of individual learners, you will have created an effective teaching and learning environment.

Activity

Research inclusion in education via the internet or in textbooks and compare and contrast the definitions. Explain how you would promote inclusion with your learners for your own specialist subject.

Table 3.3 Ways of promoting inclusion

Identifying needs	• ascertaining individual needs, learning styles and goals; • ensuring all learners can complete application and enrolment forms; for example, different languages or print sizes, electronic or hard copy; • ensuring interview notes are kept regarding any support requirements needed and these are communicated to relevant people; for example, dyslexia, epilepsy, diabetes; • ensuring learners have had access to impartial IAG to consider all their options; • ensuring programmes are offered at times everyone can attend; • exploring flexible programme delivery or blended learning approaches; • finding ways to overcome barriers such as finance, childcare, etc.; • removing barriers to enable learners to access information, staff, documents and buildings; • using initial assessment results to plan individual learning.
Planning learning	• agreeing individual learning plans/action plans; • creating resources and materials which positively promote all aspects of community and society, equality and diversity; • creating schemes of work and session plans to reflect how you will include all learners in sessions; • differentiating your teaching approaches and activities to address individual differences; for example, levels or speed of learning; • ensuring off-site visits are accessible by all; for example, transport and stairs; • ensuring the environment is accessible to all learners; • planning opportunities to develop motivation, self-esteem and confidence within your learners; • planning your delivery to meet the needs of all learning styles.
Enabling learning	• avoiding favouritism and positive discrimination; • being approachable and accessible enabling your learners to feel comfortable to talk to you; • being aware that everyone has different experiences, interests, skills and knowledge which will affect their ability to develop and learn; • carrying out an icebreaker or energiser which includes everyone; • challenging stereotyping, discrimination and prejudice as it happens;

Enabling learning *continued*	<ul><li>drawing on personal experiences of learners during each session;</li><li>embedding the functional skills of maths, English and ICT;</li><li>encouraging group discussions and activities where everyone can participate;</li><li>encouraging group work where learners can mix and participate with all members of the group over a period of time;</li><li>encouraging respect and promoting understanding of learner differences;</li><li>ensuring learners have access to facilities, resources and equipment which is appropriate for the subject and level of learning;</li><li>ensuring the language and jargon you use is at an appropriate level;</li><li>following up absences and ensuring learners have access to any missed material;</li><li>identifying where modifications or changes are needed to ensure everyone is felt included;</li><li>involving all learners within your session, using their names, using eye contact and asking individual questions;</li><li>not excluding any learner for any reason;</li><li>providing a safe and supportive environment where everyone's contribution is valued;</li><li>using a wide range of teaching and learning approaches based upon learner needs.</li></ul>
Assessing learning	<ul><li>adapting assessment activities where possible to meet any particular requirements or needs;</li><li>encouraging all learners to reach their full potential;</li><li>ensuring assessment planning is individual;</li><li>giving ongoing developmental feedback at a level to suit the learner;</li><li>recognising and valuing individual achievements.</li></ul>
Quality assurance and Evaluation	<ul><li>communicating with your team members to ensure they are aware of any learner requirements or issues;</li><li>evaluating your delivery to ensure you have included all learners fully in your session;</li><li>liaising with the awarding organisation regarding any modifications required to the learning and assessment activities;</li><li>obtaining feedback from your learners in different ways; for example, verbally, written or electronically.</li></ul>

Summary

In this chapter you have learnt about:

- identifying needs of the organisation, teachers and learners;

- initial assessment;

- potential needs of learners and points of referral;

- equality and diversity

- promoting inclusion.

Theory focus

References and further information

Clark, T (2010) *Mental Health Matters for FE: Teachers toolkit*. Leicester: NIACE.

Gravells, A and Simpson, S (2009) *Equality and Diversity in the Lifelong Learning Sector*. Exeter: Learning Matters.

Institute for Learning (2008) *Code of Professional Practice*. London IfL.

Institute for Learning (2009) *Guidelines for your CPD*. London IfL.

Race, P (2010) *Making learning happen*. London: Sage Publications Ltd.

Websites

Database of self help groups – www.self-help.org.uk

Disability Discrimination Act – www.opsi.gov.uk/acts/acts2005/ukpga_20050013_en_1

Equality and Diversity Forum – www.edf.org.uk

Open University inclusive practice – www.open.ac.uk/inclusiveteaching/pages/ inclusive-teaching/index.php

Support for adult learners – www.direct.gov.uk/adultlearning

Introduction

In this chapter you will learn about:

- schemes of work and session plans;
- differentiation;
- functional skills;
- resources;
- information and communication technology.

There are activities and examples to help you reflect on the above which will assist your understanding of how to plan your teaching and learning sessions. At the end of each section is an extension activity to stretch and challenge your learning further.

This chapter contributes towards the following: scope (S), knowledge (K) and practice (P) aspects of the LLUK Professional Standards (A–F domains) for Teachers, Tutors and Trainers in the Lifelong Learning Sector:

ASI, AS2, AS3, AS4, AK3.I, AP3.I;
BS5, BK2.I, BK2.2, BK2.4, BK5.I, BK5.2, BP2.I, BP5.I, BP5.2;
CSI, CK3.3, CK3.4, CK3.5, CK4.I, CK4.2, CP3.4, CP3.5;
DSI, DKI.I, DKI.2, DKI.3, DK2.I, DK2.2, DPI.I, DPI.2, DPI.3, DP2.I, DP2.2, DP3.I.

Schemes of work and session plans

To enable effective learning, you need to plan what you are going to teach and when. A scheme of work (sometimes referred to as a learning programme) is a document used to structure the teaching of your subject in a progressive way. It can be for a whole programme or just a unit of a qualification and can be amended at any time if necessary. It should be flexible to allow for any changes; for example, a cancelled session due to adverse weather; and detailed enough in case a colleague needs to cover for you. You will need to prepare one whether you teach groups or individuals. However, you might teach from a scheme of work that someone else has devised rather than having to create your own. If you teach the same subject as your colleagues, you could all work together to produce a standardised scheme of work. This will enable all learners to have the same learning experience no matter who their teacher is. If you meet your learners for only one session, you will not need a scheme of work, just a session plan. Individual learning programmes would be better than a scheme of work if you have learners who are all working to different requirements during your sessions.

A session plan is a detailed breakdown of each date on your scheme of work. It will outline all the teaching and learning activities, with allocated timings, assessment activities and resources required. It will also take into account the individual requirements of your learners.

Templates or pro-formas for schemes of work and session plans, and the amount of detail you are expected to enter will vary depending upon the context within which you teach. The requirements of your organisation and external inspectors will also need to be taken into account. You may be required to embed Functional Skills (covered later in this chapter) the Every Child Matters outcomes (covered in Chapter 5) and Equality and Diversity (covered in Chapter 7).

Creating a scheme of work

You will need the qualification syllabus or handbook to ensure you teach and assess all the required content. If none is available, i.e. you are teaching a non-accredited programme, you will need to devise your own programme content, along with suitable delivery and assessment material to meet the needs of your learners. When creating your scheme of work, it is useful to know something about your learners; for example, their previous knowledge and/or experience, their learning styles or any particular requirements they may have. This will enable you to plan your teaching and learning activities to achieve maximum potential. You might like to put yourself in the place of the learner when planning the order of what you will teach. This way you can see things from a beginner's perspective to ensure you keep things simple during the earlier sessions. Because you are a knowledgeable teacher, you might tend to want to achieve too much in the early stages, which could confuse your learners, even though it's very clear to you. Always ask yourself what are you going to do with your learners and why.

A rationale such as using 'five Ws and one H', *who, what, when, where, why* and *how*, will help you create your scheme of work.

Activity

Consider the five Ws and one H for the subject you will be teaching. Can you obtain all this information easily? What else will you need to know prior to creating your scheme of work? What constraints might you encounter and who can help you if you have any concerns? Obtain a copy of the documents you will be using to plan your programme and compare to Tables 4.1 and 4.3.

There are various aspects you need to consider prior to creating your scheme of work. For example, do you need to:

- obtain a syllabus to enable you to break the content down into a logical order and manageable chunks (remember what must and could be learnt depending upon how much time you have)?

- know aspects about your learners, e.g. age range, ability, prior knowledge?

- obtain any information about the subject or have any training yourself?

- allow time for an induction, initial assessment, icebreaker and ground rules in the first session?

- allow time to check if learners have had effective information, advice and guidance?

- find out what rooms, facilities and resources are available?

- embed the functional skills of English, maths and ICT?

- embed the Every Child Matters outcomes?

- plan activities and materials which can be differentiated and are inclusive?

- know the dates and times when learners will be attending?

- liaise with others?

- devise delivery and assessment materials?

- evaluate the programme delivery and your own performance?

Your scheme of work should show a variety of teaching and learning activities to suit all learning styles. Your sessions should follow in a logical order, which might not be the order printed in the syllabus. Assessment activities should be formative and summative, informal and formal (see Chapter 6).

Make sure you check all dates carefully in case there are any bank, public or religious holidays on the dates you would normally teach. The first session should include an induction to the programme and organisation, an icebreaker and the setting of ground rules (see Chapter 5). You might also need to assess prior learning in this session, or before your learners commence. All subsequent sessions should begin with a recap of the previous session and time for questions, and end with an explanation of the next session. The final session should include an evaluation activity to obtain feedback from your learners which will help you improve in future, along with details of how learners can progress, i.e. what steps they can take to further their development. You may need to check if you will have the same venue for all the sessions, and what facilities, equipment and resources will be available. The more time you take to plan your scheme of work, the easier it will be to create your session plans.

A scheme of work will help you create a logical progression of learning and should be based on the five Ws and one H rationale; for example:

- who the sessions are for, and the aim (who and why);

- objectives or learning outcomes (what);

- dates, number of sessions, and venue (when and where);

- activities, resources and assessment (how).

See Table 4.1 on page 56 for a basic example.

T041715

Table 4.1 Example – basic scheme of work showing first, second and last sessions

Programme/qualification Introduction to Information Communication Technology Level 1	Group composition 10 adults with little or no previous experience	Dates from: 8 Sept to: 13 Oct
Number of sessions Six	Contact hours 18 (3 per week) Non-contact hours 2	Venue Room 3

Aim of programme To enable learners to use a computer (for basic word processing, spreadsheets, database, internet and e-mail)

Dates	Objectives *Learners will:*	Activities and resources	Assessment
Week 1 8 Sept	• obtain and discuss information regarding the programme, organisation and assessment • switch on a computer and use a keyboard and mouse • complete an initial assessment to ascertain learning styles • discuss previous knowledge/experience and test results • describe and use ICT applications	Induction, icebreaker, ground rules, explanation of programme and organisation, initial assessment, practical and theoretical demonstration and discussion, video, differentiated activities based upon results of learning styles and to meet individual needs, explanation of next session Resources: computers, interactive whiteboard, workpacks, flipchart, handouts, exercises, quiz	Oral questions Initial assessment Observation Discussion
Week 2 15 Sept	• create, save and print documents using a word-processing program –	Recap previous session, demonstration of word processing, discussion of uses, differentiated activities and assessments, explanation of next session Resources: computers, interactive whiteboard, workpacks, handouts	Observation Oral and written questions Practical activities Gapped handout
Week 6 13 Oct	• use all programs • carry out an assessment activity • complete an evaluation form • discuss progression opportunities	Recap all sessions, explain and discuss formal assessment process, those not taking will continue with individual exercises. Complete programme evaluation, explain progression opportunities, case study activity Resources: computers, interactive whiteboard, workpacks, exercises, case study, evaluation form, assignments	Formal assignment Observation Questions

Aims and objectives

These are terms used to express what you want your learners to achieve and how they will go about this. The aim is a broad statement of intent of what you want your learners to achieve; for example, *to enable learners to use a computer*. The objective is how your learners will do this; for example, *switch on a computer and use a keyboard and mouse*.

The term *learning outcomes* could be used, depending upon the type of qualification you are teaching.

Always think of the aim as what you want your learners to achieve, and the objectives as how they will achieve it.

Objectives should always be SMART:

- **S**pecific – are they clearly defined?
- **M**easurable – can they be met?
- **A**chievable – are they possible?
- **R**ealistic – are they relevant and relate to the aim?
- **T**ime bound – can target dates/times be met?

SMART objectives enable you to teach and assess learning effectively. Always make sure the words you are using are of the right level for your learners, e.g. *list* is easier than *evaluate*. Objectives should be challenging enough to ensure learning is progressive, and inclusive to all learners.

When writing objectives, try not to use the words *know, learn,* or *understand*. These are not SMART and you would find it difficult to assess that learning has taken place.

Example

'*Learners will state the names of the Kings and Queens of England from 1066 to the present day.*'
This is better than:
'*Learners will know the Kings and Queens of England from 1066 to the present day*', *and shows you that learning has taken place.*

There are two types of objectives: behavioural and non-behavioural which relate to skills and knowledge.

Behavioural – this is when your learners can demonstrate a skill; for example, *learners will change a fuse in a plug*.

Non-behavioural – this is when your learners can demonstrate they have gained knowledge; for example, *learners will understand the law of gravity*. Non-behavioural objectives are more difficult to assess and often contain the words *know, learn* or *understand*. If you use non-behavioural objectives, try to make them SMART; for example, *learners will understand the law of gravity by explaining how it occurs*. The addition of the word *explaining* enables you to assess that learning has taken place.

Learning outcomes and assessment criteria

Another term for objectives widely used in the Qualifications and Credit Framework (QCF) is *learning outcomes*. These may be longer in terms of time taken for your learner to achieve, i.e. they might not achieve them within one session. The word *understand* often appears in the QCF learning outcomes. However, it's the assessment criteria that make them SMART. For an example, look at the learning outcomes and assessment criteria of PTLLS in Appendices 1 and 2. Although the learning outcomes and assessment criteria will have been written for you, you will still need to use aims and objectives to help you to break down your subject into more manageable topics. Learning outcomes are what *the learner will* do and assessment criteria are what *the learner can* do.

Domains of learning

Bloom (1956) stated that learning goes through five stages which can affect a person's thinking, emotions and actions. These are known as cognitive, affective, and psycho-motor domains (see Chapter 2). Attention is the first stage, leading through to a change in behaviour once learning has been successful. The stages are:

- attention;
- perception;
- understanding;
- short-/long-term memory;
- change in behaviour.

When creating your scheme of work, you need to consider which domain you want to reach.

Example

Teaching historical facts would be the cognitive (thinking) domain.
Discussing the issue of fox hunting would be the affective (emotions) domain.
Demonstrating how to change a washer in a tap would be the psycho-motor (actions) domain.

Bloom also identified six different levels of learning with associated objectives. These are:

- knowledge – list, recall, state;
- comprehension – describe, explain, identify;
- application – apply, construct, solve;

- analysis – calculate, compare, contrast;

- synthesis – argue, define, summarise;

- evaluation – criticise, evaluate, reflect.

Using Bloom's theory will help you differentiate the objectives you set to meet the correct level of your learners.

Example

Barbara teaches health and safety to a group of 20 learners. To test the knowledge of the full group she asks them to list three important Acts of legislation. To test comprehension of this legislation, she asks everyone to explain three points of each Act. Only eight learners were able to. Of those eight, she asks how they could apply the content of the Acts to a real working situation. Only two learners were able to. This shows Barbara what level her learners are at, enabling her to differentiate the teaching and learning approaches accordingly.

Table 4.2 below and table 4.3 on page 60 give examples of objectives you could use to help plan your sessions. Always be careful to choose the right objective for the level of your learners.

Table 4.2 SMART objectives

analyse;	describe;	practise;
answer;	design;	present;
assemble;	differentiate;	print;
build;	draw;	produce;
calculate;	estimate;	recall;
carry out;	explain;	recap;
change;	identify;	recognise;
choose;	illustrate;	repeat;
clarify;	justify;	select;
classify;	label;	show;
compare;	list;	sing;
complete;	make;	sketch;
construct;	measure;	solve;
contrast;	name;	state;
convert;	obtain;	summarise;
cook;	operate;	switch;
create;	organise;	use;
define;	participate;	weigh;
demonstrate;	perform;	write.

Table 4.3 Objectives which are not SMART and more difficult to assess

• accept;	• establish;	• plan;
• adapt;	• evaluate;	• praise;
• adopt;	• explore;	• prepare;
• allow;	• facilitate;	• provide;
• apply;	• familiarise;	• question;
• appreciate;	• formulate;	• rationalise;
• assist;	• gain;	• read;
• attempt;	• hear;	• reflect;
• be aware of;	• help;	• relate;
• believe;	• interpret;	• review;
• challenge;	• introduce;	• save;
• criticise;	• join;	• see;
• defend;	• judge;	• share;
• develop;	• know;	• study;
• devise;	• learn;	• suggest;
• discuss;	• listen;	• support;
• dispute;	• look;	• understand;
• enable;	• maintain;	• visualise;
• encourage;	• manage;	• volunteer;
• enjoy;	• outline;	• watch.

Creating a session plan

A session plan should be produced prior to teaching and relate to your scheme of work. Although it's very similar to the scheme of work, it is much more detailed and helps you manage the time that you are with your learners. You need to consider what you want your learners to be able to know or do by the end of the session. SMART objectives will help you focus on these and enable you to see that learning has taken place. Try not to prepare too many session plans in advance, as circumstances may change and you want the information to be fresh in your mind. Once you have a set of session plans, you can adapt them in the future for different groups of learners, rather than starting again.

Each plan should have an introduction, development and conclusion/summary; in other words, a beginning, middle, and end, with times allocated to the activities within each. Your introduction should include the aim of the session and a recap of the previous session (if applicable). This should hopefully arouse interest and link to previous learning. You could carry out a starter activity to gain attention and focus learning. If this is your first meeting with your learners, make sure you introduce yourself, explain the facilities of the organisation, the requirements of the programme, carry out an icebreaker and agree the ground rules. You can also carry out any practical matters such as taking the register, or reminding learners of any important issues.

The development stage is the teaching of your subject and should be in a logical sequence for learning to progress. Imagine you are teaching someone to make a cup of tea. You can probably do it without thinking; however, for a learner who hasn't done it before you need to appreciate just how many steps are involved. It's the same with your subject: you know it well, but for a new learner you need to break it down into smaller logical steps. You should include a variety of theory and practical approaches, activities and assessments to help maintain motivation and interest. You need to engage and include your learners by asking questions, holding discussions and carrying out activities. If you don't vary your activities the learners may become bored, lose concentration or be disruptive. Don't expect too much from them at first; they don't know what you know and will need time to assimilate new knowledge and skills. Don't forget to allow time for a break if necessary. Before concluding your session, you might like to ask questions to check knowledge (one aimed at each learner if you have time). If you have a large group, you could split them into teams and ask questions in the form of a quiz. This is a fun way of ending the session and shows you how much learning has taken place.

Your conclusion should include a summary of your original aim and relate to the objectives which have been achieved. You should allow time for any questions and to discuss any homework or other issues. You can then state what the aim of your next session will be (if applicable).

Be prepared – better to have too much than not enough. Unused material can be carried forward to another session or given as homework. Also, consider learners who may finish tasks early: can you give them something else to do?

You should always evaluate your session; this could be afterwards when you have time to reflect, and/or by making notes as you progress, i.e. if something didn't work well you could put a cross next to it on your session plan. You could note your strengths, areas for development and any action and improvements required for the future. Your plan may even change as you progress through your session to take into account the needs of your learners.

See table 4.4 on page 62 for a basic example.

There are a number of aspects to consider when creating your session plan.

- The overall aim – what you expect your learners to achieve during this session.

- Group composition – details of individual learners and needs to enable differentiation to take place.

- Objectives – how your learners will achieve your aim – how do they link to the syllabus, what order will you teach them, what timings will you allocate to each? Remember to include breaks if applicable.

- Resources – what you need to effectively teach your session – do you need to check or book anything in advance? Do you have a contingency plan?

- Teacher activities – what you will be doing. Use a variety of theory and practical approaches to meet all learning styles. You may need to embed Functional Skills, the Every Child Matters outcomes and Equality and Diversity.

Table 4.4 Example – basic session plan for the first session from the scheme of work

Teacher	A N Other	Date	8 September	Venue	Room 3
Subject/level Syllabus ref	Introduction to Information Communication Technology Level 1 Ref 1.1	**Time and duration**	6–9 p.m.	**Number of learners**	10
Aim of session	To induct learners to the programme, organisation and assessment requirements To enable learners to use a computer				
Group composition	10 adults with little or no previous experience of computers (4 female, 6 male) Initial assessment during this session will identify any prior knowledge and learning styles. One learner is dyslexic and requires handouts on pastel coloured paper. All learners will complete all planned activities, most will complete a gapped handout and some will complete an additional activity if they finish early.				

Timing	Objectives *Learners will:*	Resources	Teacher activities	Learner activities	Assessment
6.00	Obtain and discuss information regarding the programme, organisation and assessment requirements	Handouts Flipchart and paper Interactive board	Explanation and discussion	Gain knowledge Listen and ask questions	Oral questions
6.20	Complete an icebreaker	Handout	Facilitate icebreaker	Partake in icebreaker	Observation
6.40	Agree ground rules	Flipchart	Facilitate ground rules	Discuss ground rules	Discussion
6.50 (7.30 Break)	Switch on a computer and use a keyboard and mouse	Computers Workpacks Exercises Interactive board	Practical demonstration	Observe teacher Use keyboard and mouse	Oral questions
7.45	Complete an initial assessment to ascertain learning styles	Computers (online test)	Facilitate initial assessment	Complete initial assessment and learning styles test	Observation Test
8.15	Discuss previous knowledge/ experience and test results	Printed test results	Discussion	Discussion	Oral questions
8.25	Describe and use ICT applications	Interactive board (connected to internet)	Show video Facilitate practical activities	View video Use sample programs Complete gapped handout	Oral questions Observation Gapped handout
8.55	Log off computers	Flipchart	Summarise session Explain next session	Log off Hear a summary of the session Ask questions	Oral questions
9.00 End	Tidy work area and leave		Ensure computers off		

- Learner activities — what your learners will be doing and for how long — how will you keep them motivated? How will you ensure inclusion of all learners and differentiation? Do you have spare activities in case some learners finish before others? What could you remove if you run out of time?

- Assessment — how will you assess that learning has taken place?

- The next session — how will you link the sessions?

Activity

Watch one of the main news programmes on television. Notice how the presenters introduce the stories, then explain them in more detail and recap them at the end. Often there are two presenters, one male and one female, the camera shots change and there are videos and pictures to back up the stories. They will have planned and prepared well, having a contingency plan in case anything goes wrong. Did you take into account what the presenters look like and what they were wearing? Did this distract you in any way from the news?

Newsreaders have an autocue to read from; they also have the news written in paper format as a contingency plan in case anything goes wrong. They will have a script which shows the timings for the news stories and who will read them, rather like a session plan.

Your session plan should be visible at all times for you to refer to and to check how your timings are progressing. You may need to remove an activity if you are overrunning, or add something if you have spare time. You could highlight key words on your session plan to quickly glance at to help you remain focused. Or you could prepare cue cards — small pieces of card with key words or statements on that you hold in your hand or lay on a table. These will act as prompts, particularly if you have a lot of complex information to remember.

Extension Activity

Create a scheme of work for six sessions in your subject area. You may need to obtain a syllabus first; you can decide the length of each session. Create the first two session plans. Now reflect upon how easy or difficult this was, and what information you needed but couldn't obtain. How will this knowledge help you improve your planning skills and the individual needs of your learners?

Differentiation

Differentiation is about using a range of different approaches and resources to meet the needs of individuals and groups. It is very rare that a teacher has a group of learners who are all at the same level of ability, with the same prior knowledge and experience, who have the same needs. You don't have to individualise everything you do, you just need to take individual needs into account; for example, learning styles. You wouldn't help your learners if you delivered a theoretical session to a practical group of learners. Small group work is a good way to use differentiation. You could group your learners for different activities by their learning style, level of ability, level of qualification or assessment criteria, past experiences or current knowledge, etc.

> Differentiation can be defined as an approach to teaching and learning that both recognises the individuality of learners and also informs ways of planning for learning and teaching that take these individualities into consideration.
>
> (Tummons, 2010, page 93)

You could plan different activities which all your learners are capable of achieving, as well as what most or some can achieve according to their level and ability.

Example

Paul has a mixed group of level 2 and 3 learners taking a Certificate in Customer Service. He knows the full group will be able to answer questions based on the level 2 syllabus, most will be able to answer from both levels and some will be able to answer questions based on the level 3 syllabus. He has therefore devised and used a differentiated questioning technique for his group of learners.

A dyslexic learner may prefer to work with more images, have handouts printed on pastel coloured paper, wish to make an audio recording of the session to listen to afterwards or key in notes directly to a laptop. An older learner might shy away from using new technology whereas younger learners may expect to access and use it. Differentiated questioning can help support learners; for example, learners for whom English is a second language may need longer to process information or need questions rephrasing. Acknowledging and embracing the diverse nature of your learners' age, experience, culture and background should help you include all learners and bring your subject to life. Some learners may work quicker than others; giving them an extension activity could help develop and challenge their learning further, without compromising the learning of others.

Initial assessment is crucial to gain the information you need to plan effectively; however, not all your learners may reveal things during the application process or on formal documentation. If you can encourage your learners to let you know of anything that you can do to help them, you will improve their learning experience. Simply asking, *Is there anything I can do to help your learning?* should ascertain this. Alternatively, ask yourself *What can I do to give everyone a good learning experience?*

Differentiating your teaching, learning and assessment approaches should lead to more confident learners who feel included, are motivated to learn and able to achieve. While it may take longer to plan and prepare your sessions to differentiate effectively, you will find your learners are more engaged and motivated rather than being bored and uninterested.

What will you need to know about your learners to plan for effective differentiation of teaching, learning and assessment? Will this affect the initial assessment procedure? How can you differentiate the objectives and resources to take into account the needs of your learners?

Functional skills

Functional skills consist of English, maths and information and communication technology (ICT). They provide the essential knowledge, skills and understanding that will enable your learners to function confidently, effectively and independently in life and at work. Functional skills were introduced as a pilot by the government in 2007 as part of the reform of 14–19 and adult education to equip the United Kingdom with the skills it needs for the twenty-first century.

Qualifications in functional skills can be achieved at Entry level, level 1 and level 2; some of your learners may have already achieved them at school. You might not be involved in teaching the qualification requirements; however, you will need to embed elements of each within your subject. This will ensure your learners can transfer these skills to life and work.

For example:

- English – reading, writing, listening, speaking, discussions.

- Maths – approximations, estimations, calculations, measurements.

- ICT – e-mail, web-based research, word-processing assignments and reports, using spreadsheets, databases and presentation packages.

You might feel your own skills in these areas need improving, therefore you could partake in further training yourself. If you are not competent you will not set a good example to your learners. For example, if you spell words wrongly in a handout, have difficulty making calculations or can't use a computer, your learners may lose confidence in you as a teacher. The three skills should be embedded within your teaching to encourage your learners to apply them to the subject they are learning and the world of work they wish to enter.

Example

Sanjay is due to teach cookery for beginners and plans to embed the three skills as follows:

English – reading and discussing recipes, writing a list of ingredients, talking, listening and asking questions.
Maths – calculating weights and costs of ingredients, measuring amounts, estimating calorific values, cooking times and temperatures.
ICT – using a word processor to type the menu, researching healthy-eating websites, e-mailing other learners.

It's best to find naturally occurring opportunities to embed functional skills within your sessions. This will enable your learners to see it as part of the subject, not as a separate lesson in English, maths or ICT. Learners who possess functional skills should be able to progress in education, training and employment and make a positive contribution to the communities in which they live and work.

Example

Ravi teaches plumbing in a realistic working environment, and has realised that many aspects of the job naturally include functional skills. Talking to customers and suppliers and writing orders all include English. Measuring pipes, calculating the amount of materials to use and working out invoices all include maths. Researching materials on the internet, e-mailing suppliers and maintaining a diary can be carried out using ICT. Ravi therefore embeds functional skills naturally with his learners while teaching his subject.

To be effective, functional skills teaching must be realistic and relevant to enable your learners to engage with real situations, allowing them to apply the skills in their specialist subject area.

Extension Activity

How can you embed elements of the three functional skills within your specialist subject? Try them out with your learners and evaluate how effective they were. Ask your learners if they realised they were learning these skills along with the subject.

Resources

Resources are all the aids, books, handouts, items of equipment, objects and people that you can use to deliver and assess your subject. They should stimulate learning, add impact and promote interest in the subject. Resources should be accessible and inclusive to all learners, while enabling them to acquire new skills and knowledge. When using or creating resources, ensure they promote equality of opportunity, reflect diversity and challenge stereotypes. For example, text and pictures in a handout should portray all aspects of society. Resources should be appropriate in terms of level, quality, quantity and content and be relevant to the subject and the learning expected. Handouts and presentations should be checked for spelling, grammar, punctuation and sentence construction errors. You could put your name, date and organisation details on any documents to show where they originated. You may also find it useful to add a file name and version number to keep track of any changes. If you give a handout at the beginning of the session, you may find your learners fiddle with it and become distracted. If you can, issue handouts at an appropriate time and talk through the content, asking questions to ensure your learners have understood. Otherwise, issue them at the end of the session and ask learners to read them at home to help reinforce what has been covered during the session. Alternatively, to aid sustainability, you could upload handouts to a virtual learning environment (VLE) or e-mail them to your learners. Handouts can also be used as activities; for example, a gapped handout can contain sentences with missing words that learners need to fill in. These are useful to test lower-level learners, as a fun team activity or to fill in time at the end of a session. If a resource you are using is not effective with some learners, try changing the experience rather than the resource. You might need to explain the resource differently or change a group activity to become an individual one.

Examples of resources include:

- audio/visual equipment;
- books, catalogues, journals, magazines;
- computerised presentations;
- computers;
- digital cameras;
- flipchart paper and pens;
- handouts;
- interactive or electronic whiteboards;
- people: specialist speakers; colleagues;
- physical resources, models and apparatus;
- projector;
- radios/televisions;
- textbooks;
- worksheets, puzzles or crosswords.

Depending upon your subject and what is available, you may need to create your own or adapt someone else's resources. This could be a handout of useful information, an exercise, activity or worksheet or it could be a complex working model used to demonstrate a topic. If you can search the internet, you might find resources for your subject area are freely available. Whatever resources you use, it's important to ensure they cover all learning styles and meet the differing needs of your learners. Putting posters on the wall of the room will help to reinforce points. Learners may not always look at them consciously, but subconsciously will glance at them, taking in the information. You might have to acknowledge your organisation's resource constraints and make best use of what is available. You should always evaluate the effectiveness of any resources you use, to modify or change them for future use.

When designing resources, any individual needs should be taken into account; for example, dyslexia, hearing impairment, sight impairment, physical or mental disabilities. You may need to produce handouts in a larger-sized font, on different coloured paper, or ensure there is plenty of white space surrounding the text. White space is blank space on the page. You also need to consider the location, cost, challenges and benefits of using certain resources. If you are using, adapting or copying work, you will need to check you are not in breach of copyright. Using pictures as well as text and not putting too much information on a handout will help learning. If you were given one handout with a lot of written information in small text, and another with text in a larger more pleasing font with a few pictures, which one would you prefer to read? It would probably be the latter.

You may have to deal with unexpected situations which relate to resources. It is useful to have a contingency plan just in case.

Example

Jack was due to deliver a food hygiene session to a group of 12 learners at 7 p.m. He had created a computerised presentation and saved it to a memory stick. He arrived at the venue half an hour early, only to find a notice on the door stating he had been moved to another room. In the other room were two circular tables that would seat six learners comfortably, but only four chairs at each. He switched on the computer and realised the version of his presentation was newer than the one on the computer and wouldn't open. If he didn't have a contingency plan he would have been unable to deliver the session. However, because he was early he was able to locate and ask the caretaker to bring four extra chairs. He had printouts of the presentation which he could hand out to each learner, but had time to go to the office and resave the document in a previous version. Whilst there, he saved it to the organisation's hard drive which was accessible from any room, just in case a problem occurred with his memory stick.

Preparing for unforeseen circumstances comes with experience. Whenever you are due to teach a session, ask yourself, *What would I do if something wasn't available or doesn't work?* You might prepare a computerised presentation and make copies as handouts that you can give your learners. However, if you can't get copies made in time, you can still deliver your presentation and offer to e-mail a copy to your learners, upload it to a VLE, or get photocopies made later. Try not to rely totally on presentation software when teaching: use different approaches and activities to add variety.

Extension Activity

What resources could you use during your sessions to ensure both teaching and learning are effective for your subject? Review the advantages and limitations of these. Do you need to produce any resources yourself, or are there some already available you could use or adapt? Use an appropriate resource during one of your sessions and evaluate its effectiveness. If you don't know how to use the resources at your organisation ask for a training session or practise with them.

Information and communication technology

Information and communication technology (ICT) should be used whenever possible during teaching and learning to engage and stimulate your learners. It will also help raise their confidence if they haven't used ICT much in the past. Lifelong Learning UK (LLUK) believes embedding technology in learning methods has a long-term impact on learners' employment prospects and life after learning. You might deliver and assess your subject via an online program or use a blended approach of traditional teaching supported with access to technology. ICT can encompass a wide variety of activities besides e-learning using computers or accessing the internet; for example:

- audio and video clips (creating or viewing);
- calculators;
- computer programs;
- digital cameras;
- e-assessments;
- electronic brain games;
- electronic templates;
- e-mail;
- e-portfolios and e-assessment;
- interactive and online programs;
- mobile phones with various functions;
- online discussions;
- presentation packages;
- scanners;
- social networking (if appropriate);
- video conferencing;
- virtual learning environments (VLE);
- webcast, podcast, blogs, etc.

You would need to feel confident using ICT equipment yourself and may therefore need further training. You would also need to ensure everything is accessible, in working order and appropriate for your learners.

> *Some 42 per cent of adult learners most like to learn by doing practical things, a figure that is unchanged since 1998. However, now almost a quarter (23 per cent) mentioned using computers, mobile phones and the internet, not feasible options for most in 1998.*

(Campaign for Learning, 2009)

When using ICT, remember to vary your methods to reach different learning styles and address individual needs. Technology can help overcome barriers to learning; for example, pairing an experienced learner with an inexperienced learner so that someone who hasn't used it before doesn't feel alone. You also need to be careful that learners are using it appropriately, i.e. not accessing unsuitable websites or checking their e-mails while you think they are working. Some learners may be concerned about using ICT; for example, a learner with epilepsy may need regular breaks from a computer screen.

You might use equipment such as an interactive or electronic whiteboard. With a normal whiteboard, once you have written on it, you need to clean it before using it again. With the interactive whiteboard, you use a special pen directly onto the board, information is displayed and can be transferred to a computer for saving, printing, uploading to a VLE and/or e-mailing. You can open documents, move between pages and add text and pictures, link to the internet and show video clips. You can involve your learners by getting them to create and use documents, quizzes, pictures, etc.

Example

Angela is teaching a new group of learners how to use a computer. She is able to demonstrate how to use various functions by displaying each program on the interactive whiteboard, enabling everyone to see what she does. Previously, she would have had to gather the group around one small computer screen. She can also link to the internet to demonstrate how to use e-mail and access websites.

Other equipment you could use includes specialist software for delivering presentations. This would enable you to use graphics as well as text to make your presentation more visual. You can prepare your presentation in advance and save it to a disk, memory stick and/or upload it to a VLE or accessible site. Therefore as long as a computer and data projector are available, you can teach in any room. A wireless remote control is useful as it enables you to move around the room rather than stand next to the keyboard to move the slides.

Extension Activity

What ICT resources could you use within your subject? Research new and emerging technologies and create an ICT activity to use with your learners. Use the activity and then evaluate its effectiveness. If you are not yet confident with ICT, find out where you could receive training or support.

Summary

In this chapter you have learnt about:

- schemes of work and session plans;

- differentiation;

- functional skills;

- resources;

- information and communication technology.

Theory focus

References and further information

Becta (2009) *Harnessing Technology Review 2008: The role of technology and its impact on education*. Coventry: Becta.

Bloom, BS (1956) *Taxonomy of Educational Objectives: Handbook 1*. New York: Longman.

Campaign for Learning (2009) *State of the Nation Survey 2008*. London: Campaign for Learning.

Gravells, A and Simpson, S (2010) *Planning and Enabling Learning in the Lifelong Learning Sector* (2nd edn). Exeter: Learning Matters.

Hill, C (2008) *Teaching with E-learning in the Lifelong Learning Sector* (2nd edn). Exeter: Learning Matters.

Rae, P and Pickford, R (2007) *Making Teaching Work*. London: Sage Publications Ltd.

Tummons, J (2010) *Becoming a Professional Tutor in the Lifelong Learning Sector* (2nd edn). Exeter: Learning Matters.

Wallace, S (2007) *Teaching, Tutoring and Training in the Lifelong Learning Sector* (3rd edition). Exeter: Learning Matters.

Websites

Copyright – www.copyrightservice.co.uk

Every Child Matters – www.dcsf.gov.uk/everychildmatters

Functional Skills – www.qcda.gov.uk/qualifications/functional-skills/32.aspx

LLUK – Using technology in teaching – www.lluk.org/3088.htm

Qualifications and Credit Framework – www.qcda.gov.uk/qualifications/60.aspx

5 ENABLING LEARNING

Introduction

In this chapter you will learn about:

- induction, icebreakers and ground rules;
- teaching and learning approaches;
- communication;
- working with groups and individuals;
- safeguarding and Every Child/Learner Matters.

There are activities and examples to help you reflect on the above which will assist your understanding of how to teach and enable learning to take place. At the end of each section is an extension activity to stretch and challenge your learning further.

This chapter contributes towards the following: scope (S), knowledge (K) and practice (P) aspects of the LLUK Professional Standards (A–F domains) for Teachers, Tutors and Trainers in the Lifelong Learning Sector:

AS1, AS2, AS3, AS6, AK2.1, AK2.2, AK3.1, AK5.1, AK6.1, AK6.2, AP1.1, AP2.1, AP2.2, AP6.1, AP6.2;
BS1, BS2, BS3, BS5, BK1.1, BK1.2, BK1.3, BK2.1, BK2.2, BK2.3, BK2.4, BK2.5, BK2.7, BK3.1, BK3.2, BK3.3, BK3.4, BP1.1, BP1.2, BP1.3, BP2.1, BP2.2, BP2.3, BP2.4, BP2.5, BP3.1, BP3.2, BP3.3, BP3.4, BP3.5, BP5.1;
CS2, CS3, CS4, CK2.1, CK3.1, CK3.2, CP1.2, CP2.1, CP3.1, CP3.5, CP4.2;
DS1, DK1.1, DK1.2, DK2.1, DP1.1, DP1.2;
FK3.1, FP1.1, FP1.2, FP3.1, FP4.1, FP4.2.

Induction, icebreakers and ground rules

When you begin teaching a new group or an individual, there are certain points you must explain regarding your organisation, the programme/subject and the facilities available. This is known as an induction and will usually take place during the first meeting with your learners. Carrying out an icebreaker with your learners will help ensure they get to know each other and you. Establishing ground rules with your learners will help underpin appropriate behaviour and respect throughout their time on the programme.

Induction

Your organisation may have a checklist of general points for you to follow and you may need to add specific points regarding your subject and the learning environment.

It should include aspects such as:

- introducing yourself;
- dates and times of attendance;
- break times and refreshment facilities;
- checking your learners have received information, advice and guidance (IAG);
- qualification content and assessment requirements;
- a tour of the site including location of study areas, learning resources, toilets, catering venues, parking, smoking areas, etc.;
- organisational polices such as health and safety, equality and diversity, appeals and complaints;
- organisational procedures such as fire and accidents;
- an icebreaker to introduce learners to each other;
- ground rules.

There may be some administrative aspects to be completed during the first session. Don't let this take over – your learners will want to leave having learnt something interesting about the subject. If you do have a lot of information and paperwork to complete, inform your learners in advance that the first session will be the induction session, and they will not be commencing the subject until the second session. If you have any learners who commence the programme at a later date, make sure you spend time with them to cover all aspects of the induction process.

Activity

Imagine you are to begin teaching your subject to a new group of learners. Devise a checklist of the information you would need to cover. You could think back to when you started a new programme, i.e. the information you received and the questions you asked. If you are currently teaching, obtain a copy of your organisation's checklist and compare it with yours.

Giving your learners a copy of the induction checklist will act as a reminder to them of the information they have received. Often, so much information is given out during the first session that learners can easily forget some important points.

Icebreakers

Learners can be quiet, shy, nervous or apprehensive when they commence. Carrying out an icebreaker is a good way of everyone getting to know each other's name and encouraging communication to take place. Some learners may already know each other, or have carried out an icebreaker with another teacher they currently have. Knowing this beforehand will help you decide upon an appropriate and suitable icebreaker to carry out, and saves repetition. You could carry out the icebreaker before covering the induction requirements as this will encourage your learners to relax, and give them confidence to speak or ask questions in front of others.

Icebreakers can be quite simple; for example, asking your learners to introduce themselves in front of the group. However, this can be a bit intimidating if none of the learners have met before. A way round this is to form the group into pairs and ask them to talk to each other for five minutes about their hobbies, interests and reason for being there. They may find they have something in common and create a bond. You can then ask each person to introduce the person they have been talking to. People may not feel comfortable talking about themselves to a group of strangers, so another person introducing them takes this anxiety away. A good idea is to note down your learners' names when they introduce each other, on a rough sketch of a seating plan. This will help you remember their names as it's likely they will return to the same position at the next session. You could also note something about them which you could use in a future conversation. This shows that you are taking an interest in each learner.

If you don't have time for introductions, you could issue name badges for learners to wear or name cards to place in front of them. This is a visual reminder to each other, and helps you remember and use their name when speaking to them. Always introduce yourself first otherwise learners may be wondering what your name is, or whether you are their permanent teacher or just someone facilitating the icebreaker. First impressions count, therefore you need to portray that you are a professional, knowledgeable teacher who is competent and approachable.

More complex icebreakers can involve games or activities, but the outcome should be for your learners to relax, enjoy the activity, communicate and ascertain each other's names. Icebreakers help retain attention, keep motivation high and help the group to work together. All learners should be included and you should manage the activity carefully to ensure everyone can actively take part. You may wish to include yourself in the icebreaker, or just observe what is happening. If you include yourself, don't get too personal, resist the temptation to be everyone's friend and remain professional throughout.

Icebreakers can also be used during an established session, perhaps after a break to help learners refocus. These are called energisers and can be subject-specific such as a quiz or a fun activity or game which gets learners moving about. Always have a contingency plan in case anything you planned to use isn't available, or if some learners finish before others.

Whichever way you use an icebreaker or an energiser, it should be designed to be a fun and light-hearted activity to:

- break down barriers;

- build confidence;

- create a suitable learning environment;

- enable learners to talk confidently in front of their peers;

- encourage communication, motivation, interaction, teamwork and inclusion;

- establish trust;

- get the programme off to a good start;

- help learners relax;

- introduce learners to each other;

- reduce apprehension and nervousness;

- reduce intimidation.

Activity

Imagine you have a new group of 16 learners starting next week who have never met each other before. What sort of icebreaker would you carry out with them and why?

Your organisation may have icebreakers for you to use or you could design your own or search the internet for ideas. Keep your icebreaker short and simple and always evaluate how it went to enable you to modify or improve it for the future.

Ground rules

Ground rules are boundaries, rules and conditions within which learners can safely work and learn. They should underpin appropriate behaviour and respect for everyone in the group, including the teacher, and ensure the session runs smoothly. If they are not set, problems may occur which could disrupt the session and lead to misunderstandings. It is best to agree the ground rules during the first session, perhaps after the icebreaker once everyone is feeling more relaxed.

Ground rules should always be discussed and negotiated with your learners rather than forced upon them. Using an activity to do this will help learners feel included, take ownership of, and hopefully follow the rules. Some ground rules might be renegotiated or added to throughout the programme; for example, changing the break time. Others might not be negotiable but imposed; for example, health and safety requirements. These may already be listed in a learner handbook, agreement or learner contract and you would need to ensure all learners have a copy, and know that they are in addition to any rules agreed as a group.

When establishing ground rules, you need to have an idea of what needs to be imposed and what could be negotiated.

Example

Imposed ground rules:

- *no smoking;*

- *arriving on time and returning from breaks punctually;*

- *no anti-social behaviour, offensive language or swearing;*

- *respecting others' views and beliefs;*

- *following health and safety regulations;*

- *handing in work on time;*

- *not talking over someone else;*

- *paying attention and fully participating;*

- *leaving the area tidy.*

Example

Negotiable ground rules:

- *no eating or drinking during sessions;*

- *standard of dress;*

- *switching off mobile phones and electronic devices;*

- *amount of time taken during breaks.*

Whatever method you use to collate these, make sure they are not open to any mis-interpretation.

If your learners attend sessions taken by other teachers, it is a good idea to discuss with them what your group has agreed, to ensure consistency. You might also take your learners for other subjects and therefore have a core list of ground rules for all sessions, with some specific ones for each particular subject.

Ways to establish ground rules

A combination of both you and your learners working together by a process of discussion and negotiation can be used. This enables your learners to recognise what is and is not acceptable, giving them a sense of ownership and responsibility. It also enables learners to begin working together as a group and encourages aspects such as listening, compromise and respect for others. Alternatively, your learners could write down the rules individually, then discuss in pairs and join into fours to create a poster or a list on flipchart paper. One or two learners could present this to the full group and agreement can then take place. Depending upon the age of your learners, you could use the term *group contract* instead of ground rules. Ideally, the ground rules should be on display each time your group meets, and/or a typed version could be given to each learner, or uploaded to a virtual learning environment (VLE) if applicable.

Ways to maintain ground rules

Keeping the ground rules visible throughout the sessions will act as a reminder of what is not acceptable, and enable them to be amended or added to as necessary. Any learners who have commenced the programme late will be able to see them. Always refer to the rules at the beginning of the session and when a rule is broken. For example, if a learner is late, they must be reminded that it is a requirement that all lessons start promptly, otherwise they might not make the effort to arrive on time for subsequent sessions. If other learners see that you don't say or do anything, they will feel the ground rules have no value. You could also refer to the ground rules when they are not broken as positive reinforcement of good behaviour.

If a learner breaks a ground rule, you may find their peers reprimand them before you need to. You might like to ask your group to decide upon penalties or consequences for when a ground rule is broken. This could be a token penalty; for example, donating 50 pence to a group fund. Your learners can then decide what to do with the fund at the end of the programme. It could be more serious; for example, writing their name on a wall chart and allocating a point every time a rule is broken. Three points could lead to disciplinary action or removal from the session. Ultimately, you will need to find your own strategy for dealing with learners who break the ground rules, depending upon the age and maturity of the group. At the end of your session you could thank your learners for following the ground rules; this will act as a reminder of their existence.

If you can lead by example, you will help create a culture of mutual compliance which should enable effective teaching and learning taking place.

Extension Activity

What methods would you use to establish ground rules with your learners? Give examples of ground rules you would need to impose and ground rules that you could negotiate. What would you do if a learner broke a ground rule?

Teaching and learning approaches

These will depend upon the subject you are teaching, the context and environment you are teaching in and the length of each session. However, you should choose approaches which will engage, stimulate and motivate your learners. It's not about what you will teach, but how they will learn.

Formal teaching approaches include lectures, demonstrations and presentations which are usually teacher-centred, known as pedagogy. Informal approaches could include discussions, group work and practical activities and are usually learner-centred, known as andragogy. Wherever possible it's best to use a mixture of the two and vary the approaches you use. This will ensure all learning styles are met and that all learners are included and can participate.

Example

Zak teaches history in a college by lecturing to groups of learners. He feels that although he uses a computerised presentation and handouts, his learners are not actively participating in any way. He decides to make his session more practical by introducing group discussions and role plays of historical events. Several learners approach him after the session to say how much they enjoyed it and how it enabled them to put theory into practice. He now uses this approach each time to mix theory and practice. He has set up the college's virtual learning environment to encourage interaction outside of the sessions, and to upload video and audio clips for learners to access. He also finishes each session with a quiz to test knowledge gained.

Knowles is the theorist who brought the concept of pedagogy and andragogy to the fore (Knowles et al., 2005). The pedagocical approach places the responsibility for making decisions about the learning process upon the teacher, who may decide to teach the same material in the same order, at the same time to all learners. This doesn't allow any flexibility for a learner who may miss a session, or is learning slower or quicker than others.

The andragogical approach places the emphasis on the learner to take responsibility for the learning process; they can then ensure they are learning in a way that suits them. This approach also allows the teacher to adapt their teaching materials to suit each learner's progress and development. If your sessions are mainly pedagogical, try to include your learners by asking individual questions to check their knowledge or by holding discussions. Your subject should never bore your learners; you need to inspire them to maintain their motivation and interest. To help your confidence, imagine you are an actor playing a role. If you are nervous, stand tall, breathe deeply and pause for a second or two; it might seem a long time to you; however, it isn't. Focus your thoughts, relax and enjoy what you are doing. A tip if nerves do take over is to place your tongue on the roof of your mouth for a few seconds, no one will notice and you should feel better.

When commencing a session, if you are unsure what to say to gather your learners' attention, start with *Welcome to the session, today we will . . .* in a louder than normal but assertive voice. To settle your learners and focus their attention towards learning, you could use a starter activity. This could be a quiz to test knowledge gained so far, a discussion to open up thinking about the current topic, or an energiser activity focusing upon the session topic. You can then state your aim and the objectives. Always check if your learners have any prior knowledge and/or experience by asking them; you can then draw upon this during the session. Never assume your learners know or don't know something. As you teach, allow time for questioning, repeating and summarising important points. Incorporate the knowledge and experience of your learners and if you can, give relevant anecdotes to bring the subject to life. Try not to use the word *obvious*, as things are only obvious to you. Show interest, passion and enthusiasm for your subject and encourage your learners to take pride in their work. Use tone and inflection to emphasise key points and don't be afraid of silent pauses; they will give you time to refocus and your learners time to consider what you have said. If you make a mistake, don't draw attention to it, but continue professionally; your learners probably won't know any different. If you feel you are overrunning, don't be afraid to carry something over to the next session, or give it as homework. If you finish earlier than planned, make sure you have some extra activities you could use; for example, worksheets or a quiz. If particular learners finish earlier than others, you could give them an extension activity to stretch and challenge their learning further.

If you are delivering a sequence of sessions, always recap the previous session before commencing the current session. While teaching, notice the reactions of your learners; you might need to change your pace of delivery or introduce something practical to energise them. If you are demonstrating something in front of your learners, always check if they are left- or right-handed as this could change the way they see things. When they look at you, your right hand will be on their left. If you are demonstrating one-to-one, try to stand next to your learner rather than facing them. It's helpful to show a completed item if you are demonstrating how to make something; for example, a pipe weld or an iced cake.

When you are planning break times, make sure you inform your learners when these will be and for how long, otherwise they may be thinking about when they can get refreshments which will distract them from learning. If there is a break, when your learners return, ask if they have any questions. Sometimes they will have been thinking about what they learnt before the break, and would like an opportunity to clarify aspects or ask questions. If possible, walk around the room regularly to ensure your learners are not using electronic devices to communicate with their friends. If your learners are using ICT equipment as part of the session (or laptops to make notes rather than using pen and paper), make sure you agree the boundaries of what sites can or cannot be accessed, and whether they can use social networking or e-mail.

When you end your session, summarise the content, relate it to your aim and the objectives and explain what will be covered in the next session (if applicable). Plan time at the end for learner questions and clearing up; you don't want to be rushed. If you are setting any homework, be clear about your requirements and hand in dates. If you are unsure what to say to formally end your session, simply say *Thank you*. If you are due to see your learners again for another session, you could say *Thank you, I look forward to seeing you all again on. . .* Qualifications on the QCF require learners to study in their own time, known as *non-contact time*.

If you are teaching a session with a colleague, you will need to plan in advance which aspects will be covered by whom, and who will deal with any questions or behaviour issues. You will also need to plan who will introduce and close the session. Team teaching takes practice as personalities and teaching styles may differ. However, it is useful where a complex subject is being taught as different techniques of delivery can be utilised, and the experience and knowledge of the teachers drawn upon.

A mixture of different approaches within your sessions will ensure you meet all learning styles, engage your learners, retain motivation and ensure learning is successful. Never be afraid to try something new and always evaluate how it went afterwards.

Extension Activity

Make a list of at least six different teaching and learning approaches you could use for your subject to engage and motivate your learners. Consider the advantages and limitations of each and which are best suited to group or individual learning. You might like to refer to Table 5.1. for some ideas.

Table 5.1 on pages 81 and 82 contains examples of teaching and learning approaches which you might like to try with your learners. If you would like more information regarding these approaches, they are explained in detail in *Planning and Enabling Learning in the Lifelong Learning Sector* (2010) by Ann Gravells and Susan Simpson.

Communication

Communication is a means of passing on information from one person to another. It is also a manner of expression; for example, your body language, voice and the gestures you make. The first time you meet your learners they will probably make a subconscious judgement about you, and you will probably make one of them. These judgements often turn out to be wrong; therefore it is important not to make any assumptions about your learners.

Body language includes facial expressions, eye contact, gestures, posture, non-verbal signals and appearance. Your personality will show through when you are teaching and there are some aspects you might not be able to control, such as facial flushing, blinking or clearing your throat. However, some you should control, such as winking, giving a thumbs-up sign or laughing. You need to be aware not only of your own body language, but that of your learners. You need to sense what they are not saying as well as what they are saying.

Communication is the key to encouraging learner motivation, managing behaviour and disruption, and becoming a successful teacher. It should always be appropriate and effective, and to the level of your learners. If you need to write on a board or flipchart while speaking to your learners, don't do both at the same time. If you face the board, they may not hear you speak and you might miss something happening in the room.

Table 5.1 Teaching and learning approaches

Approach	Description
Activities	Tasks carried out by a group or individual, relevant to the topic being taught
Assignments	A longer-term activity based around the qualification or topic, which provides evidence of learning – can be practical or theoretical
Blended learning	Using more than one method of teaching, usually including technology. For example, a teaching session can be supported with learning materials and resources available via the organisation's VLE, with e-support/assessment from teachers as required
Buzz groups	Short topics to be discussed in small groups
Case studies	Can be a hypothetical situation, a description of an actual event or an incomplete event, enabling learners to write or discuss how they would deal with it
Coaching	A one-to-one or small group activity which involves the teacher guiding the learner – this is then followed by an observation of the learner's performance
Debates	Knowledgeable group members or guests present a case to the learners, with subsequent arguments, questions and discussions
Demonstration	A practical way of showing how something works
Dictation	Reading notes out loud for learners to write down
Discussion	Learners talk about a topic or the teacher can introduce a topic for the group to discuss
Distance learning or open learning	Learning and assessment which takes place away from the organisation offering the programme/qualification
Drawing	Illustrations to show how something works
E-learning (also see online learning)	Electronic learning – learning which is supported or enhanced using information and communication technology (ICT)
Essays	A formal piece of written text, produced by the learner, for a specific topic
Experiential tasks	Practical tasks enabling learners to act out or experience an event
Flexible learning	Learning that can take place at a time and place to suit the learner and/or using different learning approaches
Games	A fun way of learning in pairs or groups to enable problem-solving and decision-making to take place
Group work	Enables learners to carry out a specific activity; for example, problem-solving
Handouts	Written information/drawings, etc., to promote and support learning. A gapped handout will have missing words for learners to complete
Homework	Activities carried out between sessions; for example, further reading, answering questions and research
Icebreakers/ energisers	A fun and lighthearted way of introducing learners and topics, or refocusing after a break
Instruction	Formal method of teaching whereby the teacher tells or shows the learner what to do to achieve a particular skill; the learner then performs this
Interviews	Practical activity to enable learners to demonstrate skills and knowledge of a particular topic; for example, applying for a job
Journal or diary	Learners keep a record of their progress, their reflections and thoughts
Lecture	Traditional teacher-centred technique of delivering information
Mentoring	One-to-one guidance and support by someone other than the teacher, who is experienced in the subject
Micro-teaching	A session taught by the learner, usually in front of their peer group
Mind maps/ spidergrams	A visual way of organising information and making plans; learners draw a circle with a key point and branch from this with subheadings to explore and develop points further

Models	Designing and making relevant objects Life models, for example, in art classes
Online learning (also see e-learning)	Learning that takes place in a VLE via a computer connected to an intranet or the internet Asynchronous learning does not need to be accessed at fixed times or in real time Synchronous learning takes place in an environment where the teacher and learner are simultaneously present, perhaps at different locations, but communicating with each other in real time
Recognition of prior learning (RPL)	Taking into account a learner's prior knowledge, skills and achievements; as a result they do not have to retake aspects of a qualification again
Peer learning/ feedback	Learners gaining skills and/or knowledge from their peers
Practical work	A task that learners can carry out, while the teacher observes progress, usually follows a demonstration or presentation
Presentations	Similar to a lecture, with greater use of audio-visual aids and interaction with learners
Projects	A longer-term activity enabling learners to provide evidence of, or consolidate their learning towards a topic
Questions	A key technique for checking understanding and stimulating thinking. Open questions begin with who, what, when, where, why and how
Quizzes	Fun activities to test knowledge, skills and/or attitudes by the use of crosswords, panel games, etc.
Reading	Learners work from relevant texts/books/journals/internet sites, etc.
Reports	Learners produce a document to inform, recommend and/or make suggestions based on a given topic
Research	An in-depth way of finding out answers or more information regarding a topic
Role plays	Acting out a hypothetical situation
Seminars	A presentation of ideas, followed by questions and a discussion
Simulation	An imitation activity carried out when the real activity would be too dangerous
Surveys	Learners ascertain information from others regarding a particular topic, analyse and present their findings
Teaching/ training/ tutoring	Educating learners in a subject, furthering their knowledge, skills and/or attitudes
Team teaching or co-teaching	Facilitating a session with a colleague
Technology-based learning	Using relevant equipment and materials; for example, interactive whiteboards/videos/CD-ROMs/DVDs/the internet, etc.
Tests	Written questions (open, closed, multiple choice, etc.) to assess knowledge Practical activities to assess skills
Tutorials	A one-to-one or group discussion between the teacher and the learner/s, with an agreed purpose; for example, discussing progress so far
Undoing	Learners can undo or take apart an object, to learn how it was put together. An example is taking a plug apart to see how it was wired
Visiting speakers	An expert in the subject area speaks to the group
Visits/field trips	Learners visit a venue relevant to the programme or qualification
Word shower (also known as brain storming)	A list of suggestions or ideas regarding a particular theme, topic or problem which should be agreed in groups without judgements or criticisms The list can then be refined and used as a basis for other activities, usually written on flipchart paper or a board so all learners can see and take part
Worksheets	Interactive handouts to check knowledge (can also be electronic) Blank spaces can be used for learners to complete sentences Words can be circled, phrases completed, lists sorted, etc.
Workshops	Practical or simulated activities in a realistic working environment (RWE)

Successful communication includes:

- oral communication, i.e. the way you speak when explaining, describing, summarising, questioning and giving feedback — be aware of your voice projection, tone and accent and when to use pauses to gain attention or allow thinking time;

- written communication, i.e. presentations, handouts, worksheets, written feedback and progress reports — always check your spelling, grammar, punctuation and sentence construction;

- non-verbal communication, i.e. the way you act, your body language, appearance, facial expressions, eye contact, gestures, posture and non-verbal signals;

- questioning, i.e. oral or written to include all learners, preferably using open questions;

- listening skills, i.e. eye contact, not interrupting, not being judgemental;

- skills such as empathy and sympathy.

The language you use should reflect equality and inclusiveness, be relevant to the subject, not offend anyone in any way and be at the right level and pitch for your learners. You may have to practise with your voice projection, but don't shout, just speak louder and a little slower than normal and ask if learners can hear you. Don't expect your learners to remember everything first time; they don't know what you know. You should repeat or rephrase key points regularly. You might even get frustrated if asked questions regarding points you have already explained. Try not to say things like *I just told you that* or *Can't you remember what I just said?* Repeating key points will help your learners remember them. Don't embarrass a learner in front of their peer group; they may feel they can't ask you anything again. Learning occurs best in an active, not a passive, environment where communication is a two-way process. Always watch for signals from your learners to check they are learning.

Example

Olga was explaining a complex topic and noticed one of her learners, Josh, was making a strange expression, furrowing his brow as if he didn't understand. As Olga regularly uses eye contact with her learners, she quickly spotted this and asked Josh if he would like her to explain the topic again. She rephrased what she had just explained and could see from his smiling and nodding face that he now understood. To double-check his learning, she asked an open question which required an answer other than Yes or No.

Try to minimise any barriers to communication; for example, background noise, seating positions or the way you explain a topic. If a learner asks a question, repeat this when you answer it so that everyone can hear what was asked. The same applies if a learner answers a question as not everyone may hear this. Encourage your learners to ask you questions, no matter how silly they think they are; probably another learner is thinking the same but daren't ask. If you are asked something you don't know the answer to, say you will find out later and then make sure you do.

Effective listening takes place only when the person who receives the information interprets and understands it the way the deliverer intended. It can be easy to say something and think you said it in a way that your learners will understand, only to find them asking you to say it again or to rephrase it.

To help your learners hear you effectively, you should:

- speak clearly and slightly louder and slower than normal;
- not complicate your speech by including too much too soon or using too much jargon or too many acronyms;
- not lose the point of what you are trying to put across;
- remain focused;
- ask open questions regularly to check your learners are listening and under-standing.

Activity

Read the following list of words once, cover them up and then write down the words you remember.

cat	deck	table	snow	storm
sky	plant	book	smile	sky
lulu	lala	sky	plant	music
tree	bottle	money	cat	plant

Among your words are probably cat, plant, sky, lulu and lala. This is because they occur at the beginning, the end, are unusual or repeated words. Use this approach with important points when teaching, i.e. by doing something different and repeating points. Ensuring you state your aim clearly at the beginning of your session, recapping regularly and summarising at the end will help learning take place. However, don't introduce anything new in your summary as this will confuse your learners.

Extension Activity

Research different communication theories such as Eric Berne's (1964) transactional analysis and Belbin's (1993) team roles. How do these theories impact upon the role of the teacher when communicating with learners?

Working with groups and individuals

Whether you work with groups or just individuals will influence the teaching and learning approaches you choose to take. You might be teaching a broad spectrum of ages from 14 upwards, either by age group, for example, 14–16 year olds, 16–19 year olds, or a mixture of younger and older learners. Never assume or underestimate your learners' knowledge or experience and try to draw on this during your sessions.

Working with an individual on a one-to-one basis may sound like the ideal method, but if your learner is not committed to their learning, you will need to motivate them and of course keep your sessions interesting and stimulating.

When teaching groups of learners, appreciate that they are a collection of individuals, and that each may behave differently in a group situation from when they are with other individuals. Group dynamics can change; for example, when new learners commence, when the venue alters or if there are personality clashes. You will need to make new learners welcome, perhaps buddying them with another learner, or challenging behaviour and changing seating positions if there is disruption.

When facilitating group activities, make sure you give very clear instructions and a time limit. If the activity is to be carried out in small groups, knowledge of your learners will help you decide if they have the maturity to group themselves or whether you need to group them. Consider which learners will work together in case learners with strong personalities dominate and change the group dynamics. Equally, make sure quiet learners don't get left out and are able to participate. You might like to decide who will work with whom, or decide by their learning styles, levels of ability/ experience, random names, or paired activities. Don't be afraid of trying something different; for example, giving your learners responsibility for part of a session. Always remain in control and consider what you will be doing while they are working; for example, going around each group, listening, giving advice and encouragement, and reminding them of the time left.

When working with groups, you might like to consider Tuckman's (1965 and 1975) group formation theory of forming, storming, norming, performing and adjourning (see **www.infed.org/thinkers/tuckman.htm**)

Forming This is the *getting to know you* and *what shall we do?* stage. Individuals may be anxious and need to know the boundaries and code of conduct within which to work.

Storming This is the *it can't be done* stage. It's where conflict can arise, rebellion against the leader can happen and disagreements may take place.

Norming This is the *it can be done* stage. This is where group cohesion takes place and the norms are established. Mutual support is offered, views are exchanged and the group co-operates.

Performing This is the *we are doing it* stage. Individuals feel safe enough to express opinions and there is energy and enthusiasm towards completing the task.

Adjourning This is the *we will do it again* stage. The task is complete and the group separates. Members often leave the group with the desire to meet again or keep in touch.

Safeguarding and Every Child/Learner Matters

These are important aspects which form part of your responsibility as a teacher. You have a duty of care to ensure your learners are able to learn and achieve in a safe environment.

Safeguarding

Safeguarding is a term used to refer to the duties and responsibilities that those providing a health, social or education service have to carry out/perform to protect individuals and vulnerable people from harm. Following the publication of the Safeguarding Vulnerable Groups Act in 2006, a vetting and barring scheme was established in autumn 2008. This Act created an Independent Barring Board to take all discretionary decisions on whether individuals should be barred from working with children and/or vulnerable adults. In 2006, the Department for Education and Skills (DfES) produced a document called *Safeguarding Children and Safer Recruitment in Education*. This guidance was aimed at local authorities, schools and further education colleges in England who are responsible for promoting the welfare of children and young people, up to the age of 18. Following this, the document, *Safer Practice, Safer Learning* (NIACE, 2007) was produced to provide guidance in relation to adults in further education.

The Department of Health (DoH) (2000) document *No Secrets* specifies a definition of vulnerable adults.

> *A vulnerable adult is defined as a person 'who is or may be in need of community care services by reason of mental or other disability, age or illness; and who is or may be unable to take care of him or herself, or unable to protect him or herself against significant harm or exploitation'*
>
> (Department of Health, 2000)

Safer Practice, Safer Learning (NIACE, 2007) recommends that safeguarding duties extend to whole-organisation policies, values and ethos, and include all staff and learners. It is everyone's duty to promote the concepts of the safe learner.

Every Child/Learner Matters (ECM)

The Children Act 2004 provided the legal underpinning for the Every Child Matters: Change for Children programme. The term *learner*, *adult* or *citizen* is often used when teaching post-16 learners instead of *child*. Well-being is the term used in the Act to define the five Every Child Matters outcomes which should be taken into account when teaching your sessions. These are:

- be healthy;
- stay safe;
- enjoy and achieve;
- make a positive contribution;
- achieve economic well-being.

> *A curriculum underpinned by Every Child Matters requires passionate and committed teaching that offers opportunities for open ended investigation, creativity, experimentation, teamwork and performance. It should also involve real experiences and activities.*
>
> (QCA, 2008, page 2)

Ways to embed the outcomes of every Child Matters include:

- being healthy – access to drinking water and healthy food; opportunities to keep active;
- staying safe – maintaining a safe environment; health and safety training;
- enjoying and achieving – opportunities for all learners to enjoy and contribute during sessions; recognising transferable skills; achieving a relevant qualification;
- making a positive contribution – group activities, role play and teamwork; citizenship, voluntary work and work experience;
- achieving economic well-being – business and enterprise activities; inviting visiting speakers from various professions, becoming independent and autonomous, gaining employment.

Extension Activity

Find out what the policies are at your organisation for Safeguarding, and Every Child/Learner Matters. How can you ensure the environment you teach in, and the people your learners come into contact with are deemed safe?

Summary

In this chapter you have learnt about:

- induction, icebreakers and ground rules;

- teaching and learning approaches;

- communication;

- working with groups and individuals;

- Safeguarding and every Child/Learner Matters.

Theory focus

References and further information

Appleyard, N and Appleyard, K (2010) *Communicating with Learners in the Lifelong Learning Sector.* Exeter: Learning Matters.

Belbin, M (1993, 1996, 2010) *Team Roles At Work.* Oxford: Elsevier Science & Technology.

Berne, E (1964, 1973, 2010) *Games People Play – The psychology of human relationships.* London: Penguin Books.

Department for Education and Skills (DfES) (2006) *Safeguarding Children and Safer Recruitment in Education.* London: DfES.

Department of Health (DoH) (2000) *No Secrets.* London: The Stationery Office.

Department of Health (DoH) Home Office and Department for Education and Employment (DfEE) (1999) *Working Together to Safeguard Children.* London: The Stationery Office.

Gelb, MJ (1988) *Present Yourself.* New York: Jalman.

Gravells, A and Simpson, S (2010) *Planning and Enabling Learning in the Lifelong Learning Sector* (2nd edn). Exeter: Learning Matters.

Knowles, MS, Holton, EF and Swanson, RA (2005) *The Adult Learner: The definitive classic in adult education and human resource development.* Oxford: Butterworth-Heinemann.

National Institute of Adult and Continuing Education (2007) *Safer Practice, Safer Learning.* Ashford: NIACE.

QCA (2008) *Every Child Matters at the Heart of the Curriculum.* London: QCA.

Reece, I and Walker, S (2008) *Teaching, Training and Learning: A practical guide* (6th edn). Tyne and Wear: Business Education Publishers.

Wallace, S (2007) *Managing Behaviour in the Lifelong Learning Sector* (2nd edn). Exeter: Learning Matters.

Websites

Every Child Matters – www.dcsf.gov.uk/everychildmatters

Icebreakers – http://adulted.about.com/sitesearch.htm?terms=icebreakers&SUName=adulted&TopNode=99

QCF – www.qcda.gov.uk/qualifications/60.aspx

Tuckman – www.infed.org/thinkers/tuckman.htm

Introduction

In this chapter you will learn about:

- planning for assessment;
- assessment types;
- assessment methods;
- making decisions and giving feedback;
- assessment records.

There are activities and examples to help you reflect on the above which will assist your understanding of how to assess learning. At the end of each section is an extension activity to stretch and challenge your learning further.

This chapter contributes towards the following: scope (S), knowledge (K) and practice (P) aspects of the LLUK Professional Standards (A–F domains) for Teachers, Tutors and Trainers in the Lifelong Learning Sector:

AS1, AS5, AS7, AK6.1, AK6.2, AK7.1, AP1.1, AP2.1, AP7.1;
BS3, BS4, BK2.5, BK3.2, BK3.4, BK5.1, BP2.1, BP2.3, BP2.5, BP3.2, BP4.1,
CS2, CS3, CK3.2, CP3.2;
DS2, DK1.1, DK2.1, DK2.2, DP2.2;
ES1, ES2, ES3, ES4, ES5, EK1.1, EK1.2, EK1.3, EK2.1, EK2.2, EK2.3, EK2.4, EK3.1, EK3.2, EK4.1, EK4.2, EK5.1, EK5.2, EK5.3, EP1.1, EP1.2, EP1.3, EP2.1, EP2.2, EP2.3, EP2.4, EP3.1, EP3.2, EP4.1, EP4.2, EP5.1, EP5.2, EP5.5.

Planning for assessment

Assessment is a way of finding out if learning has taken place. It enables you to ascertain if your learner has gained the required skills, knowledge and/or attitudes needed at a given point towards their programme of learning. If you don't plan for and carry out any assessment with your learners, you will not know how well or what they have learnt.

Assessment can help your learners by:

- diagnosing any areas of concern to enable support to be arranged;

- encouraging discussions and questions;

- ensuring they are on the right programme at the right level;

- gaining feedback regarding what has been achieved so far, ascertaining areas for development and what is yet to be learnt and achieved;

- maintaining motivation;

- recognising what they have learnt;

- seeing any mistakes they have made; for example, spelling, grammar and punctuation in a written task or errors during their performance.

Assessment is not another term for evaluation; assessment is *of the learners* whereas evaluation is *of the programme*. Assessment is specific towards learners' achievements and how they can improve. Evaluation includes feedback from your learners and others to help you improve your own practice and the overall learner experience.

Assessments are usually:

- internally set – produced by you, or your organisation; for example, questions or assignments, which will also be marked by you;

- externally set – usually by an awarding organisation; for example, an assignment or examination. These will either be marked by you, a colleague, or by the awarding organisation that produced them.

Activity

Look at the syllabus or qualification handbook for the subject you will be assessing. What does it state your learners must achieve? These are probably expressed in terms such as 'assessment criteria'. Are any assessment activities and materials provided for you or do you have to devise your own? If none are available, find out what is required and begin to create them.

The assessment cycle

Depending upon the subject you are assessing, and whether it is academic (i.e. theory) or vocational (i.e. practical), you will usually follow the assessment cycle (see Figure 6.1 on page 91). The cycle will continue until all aspects of the qualification have hopefully been achieved by your learner, or perhaps not if they decide to leave the programme.

The cycle will then begin again with an initial assessment regarding the next subject area or unit of the qualification. Throughout the cycle, standardisation of assessment practice between assessors should take place; this will help ensure the consistency and fairness of decisions, and that you all interpret the requirements in the same way. Internal verification/moderation will also take place as part of the quality-assurance process. See Chapter 7 for further information.

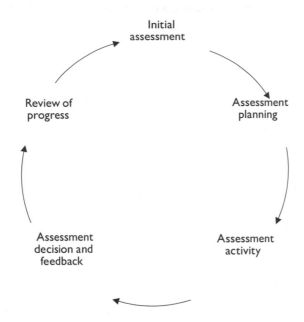

Figure 6.1 Assessment cycle

- Initial assessment – ascertaining if your learner has any previous knowledge or experience of the subject to be assessed. Relevant initial assessment activities will also give you information regarding your learners; for example, any specific assessment requirements they may have, their learning style, or any further training and support they may need.

- Assessment planning – agreeing suitable types and methods of assessment with each learner, setting appropriate target dates, involving others as necessary; for example, colleagues or workplace supervisors, and following relevant organisational guidelines.

- Assessment activity – these relate to the methods used, i.e. assessor-led; for example, observation or questioning; or learner-led; for example, completing assignments or gathering appropriate evidence of competence.

- Assessment decision and feedback – making a judgement of success or otherwise. Giving constructive feedback and agreeing any further action that may be necessary.

- Review of progress – the assessment plan can be reviewed and updated at any time until your learner completes their programme or qualification. Reviewing progress with your learners will give you an opportunity to discuss any other issues that may be relevant to their learning. Reviewing the assessment activities used will give you the opportunity to amend them if necessary.

Records should be maintained throughout all aspects of the assessment cycle.

Formal and informal assessments

Formal assessment activities will count towards your learners' achievement of their qualification; for example, successful completion of an assignment, examination or test. The criteria for these will be stated in the syllabus or qualification handbook and will probably be known as assessment criteria and linked to the learning outcomes of the qualification. Formal assessments are usually completed with certain constraints such as a time limit or the amount of resources that can be used by learners.

Informal assessment activities can take place at any time you are in contact with your learners; for example, oral questions during a tutorial review, or a quiz or discussion at the end of a teaching session. Informal activities might not always count towards your learners' achievement of their qualification, but will inform you how much learning is taking place.

Example

Cameron has taught a numeracy programme according to the syllabus, over three terms. At the end of each term, his learners take an externally-set formal test provided by the awarding organisation. To plan for this, Cameron ensured he had delivered all the required content within the time, arranged for the classroom to be formally laid out with desks in rows, and forewarned his group of the date and time of the test. Prior to this he gave them an internally-devised test to check their progress. He had also been asking questions throughout the term to check knowledge. This informal assessment ensured that his learners were ready for formal assessment.

Assessment should be a regular process; it might not always be formalised, but you should be observing what your learners are doing, asking questions and reviewing their progress throughout their time with you.

Planning

Unless all your learners are taking an examination or test on the same day at the same time, assessment should be planned for and carried out on an individual basis. Failing to plan how you are going to assess your learners may result in your learners failing the assessment activity. Assessment planning should be a two-way process between you and your learners; you need to plan what you are going to do, and they need to know what is expected of them. If your learners are all working towards the same assignment, you will still need to agree target dates for completion and discuss any specific requirements your learners may have. If your learners are to be assessed in their place of work, you will need to agree individual assessment activities and target dates. When planning for assessment, consider: *who*, *what*, *when*, *where*, *why* and *how*, to ensure both you and your learner are aware of all the requirements.

You might need to complete an assessment plan or action plan with your learners to formally document what they are aiming to achieve. This record is like a written contract between you and your learner towards the achievement of their qualification. However, it can be reviewed, amended and updated at any time.

When planning for assessment, you need to ensure what you use will be valid and reliable, and that you are being fair and ethical.

- Valid – the assessment is appropriate to the subject/qualification and assesses only what it set out to.

- Reliable – if the assessment is carried out again with similar learners, similar results will be achieved.

- Fair – the assessment is appropriate to all learners at the required level, is inclusive, i.e. available to all, and differentiates for any particular needs.

- Ethical – the assessment takes into account confidentiality, integrity, safety and security.

These aspects must always be considered carefully, to ensure you are assessing only what is necessary and relevant, at a level to suit your learners, and to ensure there is no favouritism. You also need to consider the environment in which you are assessing, i.e. that it is suitable, accessible and does not create any unnecessary barriers. Any resources you use should be relevant and effective. If you have learners with any particular requirements, you need to consider how you can help meet their needs.

Example

If you have a dyslexic learner, it may be appropriate to ask questions rather than give a written test, or have someone to scribe their responses. For a partially-sighted learner you could give papers in a larger font or use a magnified reading lamp. For a deaf learner, you could give a written test instead of an oral test. For a learner with Asperger's syndrome, you could use illustrations to support text. For some learners who might struggle with spelling and grammar, the use of a computer could help. An adapted keyboard or a pen grip could help a learner with arthritis.

Some examples of meeting your learners' needs include:

- adapting or providing resources and equipment;
- adapting the environment;
- allowing extra time;
- arranging to use another language (e.g. Welsh, British Sign Language);
- changing the date and/or time;
- liaising with others who could offer advice or technical support;
- maintaining constant contact and support; for example, via e-mail;

- providing specialist support staff;

- providing the assessment information in an alternative format;

- using a different location which is more accessible;

- using different assessment types and methods to suit learning styles;

- using ICT and new and emerging technologies;

- using larger print, Braille, or other alternative support mechanisms.

Always check with your awarding organisation to ensure you are following their regulations and requirements before making any changes. You may need to communicate with others who have an interest in your learners' progress; for example, their employer, or others who also teach or assess your learners.

Assessment planning should be inclusive to all, and always be specific, measurable, achievable, realistic and time-bound (SMART).

- **S**pecific – the activity relates only to the qualification and assessment criteria being assessed and is clearly stated.

- **M**easurable – the activity can be measured against the qualification and assessment criteria, allowing any gaps to be identified.

- **A**chievable – the activity can be achieved at the right level.

- **R**ealistic – the activity is relevant and will give consistent results.

- **T**ime bound – target dates and times are agreed.

You will need to take into account the possible contribution of any other people involved in the assessment process; for example, colleagues, managers, supervisors or witnesses. You should always inform your learners when they can expect to receive any feedback or formal recognition of their achievements.

Extension Activity

Create an assessment plan or action plan for an individual learner, which leads to a logical progression of achievement over a period of time. Ensure it is SMART and that the chosen assessment criteria can be achieved at the right level.

Assessment types

Assessment types include initial (at the beginning), formative (ongoing) and summative (at the end). Depending upon the subject you are assessing and the relevant awarding organisation's requirements, you might carry out various types of assessment with your learners which could be on a formal or informal basis.

Initial assessment

This should take place prior to or when your learners commence a particular programme or subject; see Chapter 3 for further information. A quick question during your session, *Has anyone done this before?*, will soon give you some idea of what your learners already know. Relevant initial assessment activities will also give you information regarding your learners; for example, any specific assessment requirements or needs they may have, their learning style, or any further training and support they may need.

Formative assessment

Formative assessment should take place continually throughout your learners' time with you and allow for development to take place. Simply asking questions and observing actions can help you give ongoing feedback to enable your learners to develop further, before a summative or final assessment takes place.

Assessing your learners on a formative basis will enable you to see if they are ready prior to a summative assessment. You could use activities, quizzes and short tasks for them to carry out which would make the assessment process more interesting and highlight any areas which need further development. If you are assessing a programme whereby the activities are provided for you, for example, examinations or tests, there is often the tendency to teach purely what is required for them to achieve a pass. Teaching to pass tests or examinations does not maximise a learner's ability and potential.

Summative assessments

Summative assessments usually occur at the end of a programme, topic, unit or full qualification. They can often be quite stressful to learners and sometimes lead to a fail result even though the learner is quite capable under other circumstances. However you assess your learners, you must always make sure you are assessing only what needs to be assessed, i.e. the qualification requirements.

Extension Activity

Design a formative assessment activity that you could use with your learners. You could create an assignment, a crossword, a quiz, a role play or something else which is relevant to their level and ability. Carry out the activity with your learners and evaluate how successful it was. What changes would you make and why?

Assessment methods

The methods you use will depend upon whether you are assessing knowledge, skills or attitudes. Whether the awarding organisation states which methods you must use, or whether you choose your own, you need to treat each learner as an individual, take into account equality and diversity and any particular learner requirements.

Formal and informal assessment

Assessment methods are different from assessment types. A method is how the assessment type will be used and will be classed as formal or informal.

Formal assessment methods include:

- assignments;
- case studies;
- essays;
- examinations;
- multiple-choice questions;
- observations;
- professional discussions;
- projects;
- tests;
- witness testimonies.

Informal assessment methods include:

- discussions;
- gapped handouts;
- journals/diaries;
- peer feedback;
- puzzles, crosswords and quizzes;
- questions – oral and written;
- role plays.

All assessment methods should be suited to the level and ability of your learners. A level 1 learner might struggle to maintain a journal; a level 2 learner may not be mature enough to accept peer feedback. A level 3 learner may feel a puzzle is too easy, and so on.

Questions are often the best way to assess knowledge, and observations are a good way to assess skills and attitudes.

Questioning techniques

If you are asking questions verbally to a group of learners, ensure you include all learners. Don't just let the keen learners answer first as this gives the ones who don't know the answers the chance to stay quiet. Ask a question, pause for a second and then state the name of a learner who can answer. This way, all learners are thinking about the answer as soon as you have posed the question, and are ready to speak if their name is asked. This is sometimes referred to as 'pose, pause, pounce'. To ensure you include everyone throughout your session, you could have a list of their names handy and tick each one after you have asked them a question. When asking questions, use only one question in a sentence, as more than one may confuse your learners. Try not to ask *Does anyone have any questions?*, as often only those who are keen or confident will ask, and this doesn't tell you what your learners have learnt. Try not to use questions such as *Does that make sense?* or *Do you understand?*, as your learners will often say *Yes* as they feel that's what you expect to hear.

Try to use open questions which require an answer to demonstrate knowledge and understanding. For example, *How many days are there in September?* This ensures your learner has to think about their answer. Using a closed question such as *Are there 30 days in September?* would give only a yes/no answer which doesn't show you if your learner has the required knowledge. Open questions usually begin with *who, what, when, where, why* and *how*.

If you are having a conversation with your learner, you can ask probing questions to ascertain more information. These can begin with: *Why was that?* You can prompt your learner to say more by asking *What about. . .?* You can also clarify what your learner is saying by asking *Can you go over that again?*

If you have to write your own questions for learners, think how you will do this, i.e. short questions, essay-style questions, open, closed or multiple choice. If you are giving grades, e.g. A, B, C, or pass/merit/distinction, you need clear grading criteria to follow to make sure your decisions are objective, otherwise your learners may challenge your decisions.

Multiple-choice questions should have a clear question and three or four possible answers. The question is known as the stem, the answer is called the key and the wrong answers are called distracters. Answers should always be similar in length and complexity. Answers should not be confusing, and there should be only one definite key.

Example

Summative assessment is always:

A before the programme commences
B at the beginning of the programme
C in the middle of the programme
D at the end of the programme

You will see that all the answers contain a similar amount and type of words. None of the answers contains a clue from the question. A, B and C are the distracters and D is the correct answer (the key).

If you are using the same questions for different learners at different times, be careful as they may pass the answers to each other. You may need to rephrase some questions if your learners are struggling with an answer, as poor answers are often the result of poor questions. For essay and short-answer tests you should create sample answers to have something to compare with. Be careful with the use of jargon – just because you understand doesn't mean your learners will.

You need to be aware of plagiarism, particularly now that so much information is available via the internet. Learners should take responsibility for referencing any sources of all work submitted, and may be required to sign an authenticity statement. If you suspect plagiarism, you could type a few of their words into an internet search engine or specialist program and see what appears. You would then have to challenge your learner as to whether it was intentional or not, and follow your organisation's plagiarism procedure.

Observation

Observing your learners enables you to see just how well they are doing. Let your learner make a mistake (if it is safe) rather than interrupt them as they will learn from their mistakes. You can then ask them afterwards to see if they realised. You can also observe group work and presentations; this can encourage learners to give peer feedback. You would need to make a decision as to the contribution of each learner if their work was part of a group activity. Observations are useful in the work-place to assess your learners' competence, skills and attitudes. You can always follow an observation with questions to check knowledge.

Extension Activity

Review and evaluate the assessment activities that you could use for your particular subject. Are they pitched at the right level and will they fully assess the criteria? What do you consider to be their strengths and limitations?

Table 6.1 on pages 99 and 100 lists some of the assessment methods you might wish to use. A more comprehensive list can be found in the companion book *Principles and Practice of Assessment in the Lifelong Learning Sector* by Ann Gravells.

Table 6.1 Assessment methods

Method	Description	Strengths	Limitations
Assignments	Several activities or tasks to cover theory and practice	Can challenge your learner's potential or consolidate learning A well-written project will help your learner provide evidence of knowledge, skills and attitudes	Ensure all aspects of the syllabus have been taught beforehand Must be individually assessed and written feedback given
Discussions/debates	Learners talk about a relevant subject which contributes to the assessment criteria	All learners can participate Allows freedom of viewpoints, questions and discussions	Assessor needs to keep the group focused and set a time limit Some learners may not get involved, others may take over
E-assessments /online assessments	Assessment using information and communication technology (ICT)	Can take place at a time to suit learners Participation is widened Results can be instantly generated Less paperwork for the assessor	Learners need to be computer literate Authenticity of learner's work may need validating Technical support may be required
Essays	Formal pieces of written text	Useful for academic subjects Can check your learner's language and literacy skills at specific levels	Marking can be time-consuming Plagiarism can be an issue Learners need good writing skills
Examinations	Formal tests which should be carried out in certain conditions	Can be open book, or open notes, enabling learners to have books and notes with them	Some learners may be anxious Learners may have been taught purely to pass expected questions, therefore they may forget everything afterwards
Journal/diaries	Learners keep a record of their progress, their reflections and thoughts, and reference these to the assessment criteria	Develop self-assessment skills Relate theory to practice Help assess language and literacy skills Useful for higher-level programmes	Should be specific to the learning taking place and be analytical rather than descriptive Can be time-consuming to read
Observations	Watching learners perform a skill	Enable skills to be seen in action Can assess several aspects of a qualification at the same time (holistic)	Timing must be arranged to suit your learner, communication needs to take place with others (if in your learner's working environment)
Peer assessments	Learners giving feedback to each other	Promote learner involvement Activities can often correct misunderstandings and consolidate learning without intervention by the assessor	There may be personality clashes resulting in subjective decisions Need careful management and training in how to give feedback
Portfolios of evidence	Formal records of evidence (manual or electronic) to meet the assessment criteria	Can be compiled over a period of time Learner-centred, promotes autonomy	Authenticity and currency to be checked Tendency for learners to produce too much Can be time-consuming to assess

Method	Description	Strengths	Limitations
Professional discussions	Conversations between the assessor and learner based around the assessment criteria	Ideal way to assess aspects which are more difficult to observe, or to complete any identified gaps from other assessments	A record must be kept of the discussion Need careful planning
Puzzles, quizzes, word search, crosswords, etc.	Fun ways of assessing learning in an informal way	Useful backup activity if learners finish an activity earlier than planned Good way to assess progress of lower-level learners and retention of facts	Can seem trivial to mature learners Does not assess your learner's level of understanding or ability to apply their knowledge to situations
Questions – oral or written	A key technique for assessing understanding and stimulating thinking	Can challenge your learner's potential Can test critical arguments or thinking and reasoning skills	Questions must be unambiguous If the same questions are used with other learners, they could share the answers Expected responses need to be produced
Recognition of prior learning (RPL)	Assessing what has previously been learnt to find a suitable starting point for further assessment	Ideal for learners who have achieved aspects of the programme already No need for learners to duplicate work, or be reassessed	Checking the authenticity and currency of the evidence provided is crucial Can be time-consuming for both your learner to prove, and you to assess
Role plays	Learners act out a hypothetical situation	Encourage participation Can lead to debates Link theory to practice	Can be time-consuming Clear role must be defined Not all learners may want, or be able to participate
Self-assessments	Learners decide how they have met the criteria, or are progressing at a given time	Promote learner involvement and personal autonomy Encourage learners to check their own work before handing it in	Learners may feel they are doing better than they actually are
Tests	Formal assessment situations	Cost-effective method as the same test can be used with large numbers of learners Some test responses can be scanned into a computer for marking and analysis	Needs to be carried out in supervised and timed conditions Can be stressful to learners Feedback may not be immediate Learners taking a test before others may communicate the answers
Witness testimonies	Statements from a person who knows the learner	The witness can confirm competence or achievements, providing they are familiar with the assessment criteria; for example a workplace supervisor	The assessor must confirm the suitability of the witness and check the authenticity of any statements
Worksheets and gapped handouts	Interactive handouts to check knowledge (manual or electronic) Blank spaces can be used for learners to fill in the missing words	Informal assessment activity which can be carried out individually, in pairs or groups Useful for lower-level learners and differentiation	Mature learners may consider them inappropriate Too many worksheets can be boring, learners might not be challenged enough

Making decisions and giving feedback

Making decisions

The decisions you make regarding your learners' progress, can affect them both personally and professionally. It's important to remain factual about what you have assessed and to be objective with your judgements. You should never compromise and pass a learner just because you like them, feel they have worked hard or are under pressure to achieve targets.

All assessment activities should be valid, authentic, current, sufficient and reliable (VACSR).

- **V**alid – the work is relevant to the assessment criteria.

- **A**uthentic – the work has been produced solely by the learner.

- **C**urrent – the work is still relevant at the time of assessment.

- **S**ufficient – the work covers all the assessment criteria.

- **R**eliable – the work is consistent across all learners, over time and at the required level.

When making a formal decision, you will need to complete relevant records to prove that assessment took place. Usually, you will keep the original document and give your learner a copy.

Reviewing progress

It is important to review your learners' progress regularly, as this gives you the opportunity to discuss on a one-to-one basis how they are progressing, what they may need to improve and what they have achieved. Often, this is formally documented and signed by both parties so that records of the discussion are maintained.

Reviews are a good opportunity to carry out formative assessments in an informal way. They also give your learner the chance to ask questions they might have been embarrassed about asking in a group situation.

Giving feedback

All learners need to know how they are progressing, and what they have achieved. Feedback should help reassure, boost confidence, encourage and motivate. Feedback can be given formally, i.e. in writing, or informally, i.e. verbally, and should be given at a level which is appropriate for each learner. Feedback can be direct, i.e. to an individual, or indirect, i.e. to a group. It should be more thorough than just a quick comment and should include specific facts which relate to progress, success or otherwise in order to help your learners develop.

Activity

Think back to the last time you received feedback from someone for something you did. Was this feedback constructive? Did it leave you feeling motivated and good about what you had done? Or did it leave you feeling demotivated and not willing to continue?

If possible, feedback should be a two-way process, allowing a discussion to take place to clarify any points. If you are giving verbal feedback, be aware of your body language, facial expressions and tone of voice. Don't use confrontational words or phrases likely to cause offence such as racist or stereotypical remarks. Take into account any non-verbal signals from your learners; you may need to adapt your feedback if you see they are becoming uncomfortable. If you are giving written or electronic feedback consider that how your learner reads it may not be how you intended it.

Feedback should never just be an evaluative statement like *Well done*, or *That's great you've passed*. This doesn't tell your learner what was done well, or was great about it. Your learner will be pleased to know they have passed; however, they won't have anything to build upon for the future.

Descriptive feedback lets you describe what your learner has done, how they have achieved and what they can do to progress further. It enables you to provide opportunities for your learner to make any adjustments or improvements to reach a particular standard.

Skinner (1968), a behaviourist theorist, argued that learners need to make regular active responses. These responses need immediate feedback with differential follow-ups; depending upon whether or not they were correct. Without immediate feedback, especially when the response is wrong, your learner will carry on making the same mistake thinking they are right. They will then have to unlearn their response. Time can be wasted by learners unlearning their wrong responses instead of learning new behaviours.

Most people need encouragement, to be told when they are doing something well and why. When giving feedback it can really help your learner to hear first what they have done well, followed by what they need to improve, and then end on a positive note to keep them motivated. This is known as the 'praise sandwich'. Often, the word *but* is used to link these points; replacing this with the word *however* is much easier for your learner to accept.

Example

Start with something positive, e.g. 'George, I really liked the way you delivered your presentation, you came across as very confident.'
Link with 'however' to anything that needs improving, e.g.'. . . however, I feel if you had faced the group a bit more rather than looking at the screen I could have heard your voice better.'
End on a positive note, e.g. 'It was a very interesting topic and I feel I've learnt something new.'

Using your learner's name makes the feedback more personal, and making the feedback specific enables your learner to see what they need to do to improve. You will need to find out from your organisation how they require you to give feedback; for example, writing in the first, second or third person. You also need to know whether it should be given verbally and/or written; formally or informally; how much detail should be given; what forms must be completed; and what records must be maintained.

The advantages of giving constructive feedback are that it:

- creates opportunities for clarification and discussion;

- emphasises progress rather than failure;

- helps improve confidence and motivation;

- identifies further learning opportunities or any action required.

You could ask for feedback from your learners as to how they felt about the assessment process. This will help you improve your own skills or to pass on information to the Awarding Organisation if necessary.

Extension Activity

Research different feedback methods; for example, evaluative and descriptive; constructive and destructive; objective and subjective. Consider the strengths and limitations of each and decide which methods are best suited to your subject along with the reasons why.

Assessment records

Records must be maintained to satisfy your organisation's internal quality-assurance systems, and external regulators such as Ofsted, and the awarding organisation's requirements. Assessment records must show an audit trail of your learners' progress from commencement to completion and are usually kept at your organisation for three years. If a learner loses their work, without any assessment records you have nothing to show that you actually assessed it. If you are teaching a programme which does not lead to a formal qualification, i.e. non-accredited, you will still need to record learner progress. This is known as recognising and recording progress and achievement (RARPA).

Records must be up to date, accurate, factual and legible whether they are stored manually or electronically. If you are saving to a computer, always ensure you have a backup copy in case any data are lost. You must always maintain confidentially and follow relevant legislation such as the Data Protection Act (1998 and 2003), which is mandatory for all organisations that hold or process personal data. The Freedom of Information Act (2000) gives your learners the opportunity to request to see the information your organisation holds about them. Keeping full and accurate factual records is also necessary in case one of your learners appeals against an assessment decision. If this happens, don't take it personally; they will be appealing against your decision, not you.

Assessment records include:

- action plans;

- appeals;

- assessment feedback;

- assessment grades;

- assessment plans;

- attendance records;

- copies of certificates to prove achievement;

- diagnostic test results;

- initial assessment results;

- learning styles test results;

- observation reports and checklists;

- progress reports to employers or parents/guardians;

- records of achievement;

- skills' audit results;

- tracking sheets;

- tutorial reviews;

- witness testimonies.

Extension Activity

Make a list of all the assessment records you would use for your subject. What improvements could you make to simplify them, whilst maintaining a full audit trail of learner achievement? What organisational or regulatory requirements must you follow regarding assessment records and why?

Summary

In this chapter you have learnt about:

- planning for assessment;
- assessment types;
- assessment methods;
- making decisions and giving feedback;
- assessment records.

Theory focus

References and further information

Gravells, A (2011) *Principles and Practice of Assessment in the Lifelong Learning Sector* (2nd edn). Exeter: Learning Matters.

Ofqual (2009) *Authenticity – a guide for teachers*. Coventry: Ofqual.

Skinner, BF (1968) *The Technology of Teaching*. New York: Appleton, Century and Crofts.

Tummons, T (2007) *Assessing Learning in the Lifelong Learning Sector*. Exeter: Learning Matters.

Websites

Assessment guidance booklets –
www.sflip.org.uk/assessment/assessmentguidance.aspx

Assessment methods in higher education –
www.brookes.ac.uk/services/ocsd/2_learntch/methods.html

Assessment tools (literacy, numeracy, ESOL, dyslexia) – www.toolslibrary.co.uk

Chartered Institute for Educational Assessors – www.ciea.org.uk

Data Protection Act (1998 and 2003) –
http://regulatorylaw.co.uk/Data_Protection_Act_2003.html

Freedom of Information Act (2000) –
www.opsi.gov.uk/Acts/acts2000/ukpga_20000036_en_1

Initial assessment –
www.excellencegateway.org.uk/page.aspx?o=nav-resources&node=8436

Learning styles – www.vark-learn.com

Ofsted – www.ofsted.gov.uk

Plagiarism – www.plagiarism.org and www.plagiarismadvice.org

RARPA – http://archive.niace.org.uk/projects/RARPA/Default.htm

Introduction

In this chapter you will learn about:

- quality assurance;
- evaluation;
- self-reflection and learning journals;
- continuing professional development;
- progression.

There are activities and examples to help you reflect on the above which will assist your understanding of what quality assurance is and how to evaluate yourself and the programmes you have taught. At the end of each section is an extension activity to stretch and challenge your learning further.

This chapter contributes towards the following: scope (S), knowledge (K) and practice (P) aspects of the LLUK Professional Standards (A–F domains) for Teachers, Tutors and Trainers in the Lifelong Learning Sector:

AS4, AS7, AK4.2, AK4.3, AK7.2, AK7.3, AP4.2, AP4.3, AP7.2, AP7.3;
BS2, BK2.6, BP2.6, BP2.7;
CSI, CS3, CS4, CKI.I, CK3.4, CK4.I, CPI.I, CP3.3, CP3.4, CP4.I;
DS3, DK3.I, DK3.2, DP2.I, DP3.2;
ES4, EK4.2, EK5.I, EP4.2, EP5.I;
FS3, FP3.I.

Quality assurance

All programmes should follow a quality assurance system to ensure they are being delivered and assessed fairly, consistently and accurately. You might not be involved with all aspects of quality assurance at your organisation; however, they will impact upon your role, therefore you should familiarise yourself with the requirements. Quality assurance can be internal, i.e. issuing learner surveys, updating policies and procedures and observing teaching sessions. It can also be external, i.e. inspectors, auditors and verifiers visiting to check compliance.

Information gained from aspects of quality assurance must lead to improvements for your learners, yourself and your organisation.

Activity

Have a look at the example in Figure 7.1 below of a quality assurance cycle and describe how each aspect could impact upon your role as a teacher.

Prior to programme commencing

Advertising, marketing and recruitment is planned.
Prospectus, website and leaflets are updated.
Last year's targets are reviewed.
This year's targets are set.
Policies and procedures are reviewed.
Quality systems are reviewed.
Self-assessment report is updated.

Programme completes

Final learner surveys are issued and analysed.
Retention, success and achievement data are compared with original targets.
Complaints/appeals are analysed.
Inspection, external verification/ moderation reports are analysed.
Team meetings take place to evaluate each programme.

Planning programme delivery

Internal approval to offer programmes is based on local market information, demand and funding.
Results from previous surveys, audits, inspections and reports help plan improvements.
Staff training takes place.
Learner interviews and initial assessments take place.
Resources for existing programmes are revised based on feedback.

Programme continues

Retention is monitored.
Teaching practice is observed.
Ongoing surveys are issued and analysed.
Standardisation of practice takes place.
Internal/external verification/ moderation takes place – action points are followed up.
Complaints/appeals responded to.
Learner reviews take place.
Staff appraisals take place.

Programme commences

Team meetings take place to discuss programme issues and policies, e.g. Equality and Diversity and Safeguarding.
Enrolment and attendance figures are monitored.
Staff CPD is ongoing
Inspections, audits and observations begin to take place.
Liaison with external bodies is ongoing.

Figure 7.1 Example of a quality assurance cycle

Standardisation of practice

Standardisation enables consistency and fairness of teaching and assessment. If more than one person is teaching and/or assessing the same qualification, it is important that they all agree how to interpret the requirements, deliver the content and make assessment decisions. Attending a standardisation meeting is also an opportunity to develop and share good practice and be part of a team. It is best to meet prior to the programme commencement to discuss the qualification requirements, design the scheme of work, assessment activities and any resources. Once assessments have taken place, another meeting can be held to bring examples of assessment decisions to compare and discuss. Double or blind marking can take place, whereby another assessor marks the work (with or without seeing the original grade) to ensure consistency and fairness.

Internal verification and moderation

Internal verification should be carried out by another member of staff who is qualified and experienced in your subject area. They will validate a sample of your decisions and give you feedback and advice. If a problem is found with a learner's work, they will have the chance to correct it. Another form of quality assurance is internal moderation. With this method, if the internal moderator finds problems with a particular area sampled, all the learners' work for this area will need to be re-checked.

Observations

You will probably be observed at some time when you are teaching or assessing. This might be by your internal verifier, line manager, external verifier, inspector or mentor. You should be notified beforehand and it's important to have all your records available, i.e. scheme of work, session plans, assessment results, register, etc. You should receive feedback which will help you improve your future practice.

Extension Activity

If you are currently teaching, ask a colleague or your mentor to observe one of your sessions. Use the feedback as an opportunity to improve your practice. Then ask if you could observe one of their sessions.

If you are not currently teaching, ask your PTLLS teacher if they could put you in touch with someone who would be willing to let you observe them. Seeing how an experienced teacher delivers their subject should give you some useful ideas for when you do become a teacher. The checklist in Appendix 3 should prove helpful.

Evaluation

Whichever type of programme you teach, short- or long-term, it is important to evaluate the teaching and learning process. This should be an ongoing procedure throughout all aspects of the teaching and learning cycle. It will help you realise how effective you were and what you could change or improve; for example, using different types of resources. It will also help you identify any problem areas, enabling you to do things differently next time. Using feedback from others, information and data is the best way to evaluate the programme you have taught. Never assume everything is going well just because you think it is.

Obtaining feedback

Feedback can come from surveys and questionnaires, reviews, appraisals and informal and formal discussions and meetings. Other information to help you evaluate your programme includes statistics such as retention, success and achievement rates which can affect the amount of funding received. All feedback should help evaluate whether teaching and learning have been successful (or not) as well as help you to improve your own practice and inform future planning.

If you have taught a one-day or short programme, you might give your learners a questionnaire at the end. Always build in time to your session for this to take place, otherwise your learners may take away the questionnaire and forget to return it. It could contain closed questions such as *Were the teaching and learning approaches suitable? Yes/No,* or open questions such as *How did you find the teaching and learning approaches?* The latter is best as you should gain more information. When issuing questionnaires, decide whether you want the responses to be anonymous or not, as you might gain more feedback if learners know they are unidentifiable.

You might decide to use a mixture of open and closed questions. Open questions always require a full response and give you *qualitative* data to work with; closed questions get only a yes or no answer and give you *quantitative* data. If you use a closed question, follow this up with an open question to enable you to obtain further information.

Example

1. *Did the programme fulfill your expectations? Yes/No*
   How did it achieve this?
2. *Were the teaching methods and resources appropriate? Yes/No*
   Why was this?
3. *Was the venue suitable? Yes/No*
   What did/didn't you like about it?
4. *Did you enjoy your learning experience? Yes/No*
   What did/didn't you like?
5. *Have you gained the skills and knowledge you expected to? Yes/No*
   What improvements would you recommend for the future?

There are many ways of writing questions to gain different types of responses. A closed question could be followed by a response scale of 1–5 for learners to circle (1 being no or low, 5 being yes or high); for example:

Did the programme fulfill your expectations?   1   2   3   4   5

The tendency might be to choose number 3 as it is in the middle. Removing a number makes the response more definitive one way or the other; for example:

Did the programme fulfill your expectations?   1   2   3   4

Instead of numbers, you could use smiley faces for learners to circle. For example:

Did the programme fulfill your expectations?   ☹   ☺   ☺

Having fewer options should help to gain a realistic response. Whatever you decide to ask, make sure you keep your questions simple: don't ask two questions in one sentence or use complicated jargon, allow space for written responses and thank your learners for their contributions. Always analyse the responses and inform your learners how their contributions have led to changes and improvements.

Talking to your learners informally will help you realise how successful teaching and learning has been. This can be done during reviews, at break times or before or after your sessions. Your learners are the best judges of whether they are getting what they feel they need. If given the opportunity, they may give you more feedback in an informal situation.

If you are teaching a longer programme, it is useful to obtain feedback part-way through, as well as at the end. This will enable you to make any necessary changes. Evaluation and feedback can contribute to your organisation's quality cycle by helping improve the service given to learners.

Extension Activity

Design a short questionnaire that you could use with your own learners. Consider what information you would like to know and why, and then write your questions carefully. If you are in-service, compare your questionnaire with ones currently used in your organisation. Use the questionnaire with your learners, collate the responses and write a short report as to what changes you would make as a result of the feedback gained.

Self-reflection and learning journals

When teaching, you are also learning about yourself. For example, how you react to different situations or learners, how patient you are and what skills you may need to develop. You may also decide you need further training to improve your subject knowledge and/or literacy and numeracy skills. Self-reflection should take place after each session you teach, or any significant incident, to consider what went well and what could be improved. For example, you could ask yourself if you used eye contact with each learner and addressed everyone by name at some point during the session. If your answer is *No* then next time ensure that you do. Another question to ask yourself is, *How do I know that learning has taken place?* If you can't answer this, you will need to make some changes to your teaching and assessment methods.

Reflection is often just your thoughts which can be positive or negative but can take into account any feedback you have received. It is useful to keep a learning journal to note anything important; you can then refer to this when planning your future development or preparing your teaching sessions. Reflection is about becoming more self-aware, which should give you increased confidence and improve the links between the theory and practice of teaching and learning.

A straightforward method of reflection is to have the experience, then describe it, analyse it and revise it (EDAR). This method should help you think about what has happened and then consider ways of changing and/or improving it. See Table 7.1 on page 112 for an example.

Experience → Describe → Analyse → Revise
EDAR

- *Experience* – a significant event or incident you would like to change or improve.

- *Describe* – aspects such as *who* was involved, *what* happened, *when* it happened and *where* it happened.

- *Analyse* – consider the experience deeper and ask yourself *how* it happened and *why* it happened.

- *Revise* – think about how you would do it differently if it happened again and then try this out if you have the opportunity.

Reflection should become a part of your everyday activities, enabling you to analyse and focus on things in greater detail. All reflection should lead to an improvement in practice; however, there may be events you would not want to change or improve as you felt they went well. If this is the case, reflect as to why they went well and use these methods in future sessions. If you are not able to write a reflective journal, mentally run through the EDAR points in your head when you have time. As you become more experienced at reflective practice, you will see how you can make improvements.

There are various theories regarding reflection. Schön (1983) suggests two methods:

- reflection in action;

- reflection on action.

Reflection in action happens at the time of the incident, is often unconscious and allows immediate changes to take place.

Example

Sarah was teaching a group of adults attending college as part of a day-release business studies programme. She had underestimated how fast they would learn as they were getting through the day's activities much quicker than she had originally planned. At break time, she obtained some extra activities which she then used with the group. This enabled her to reflect immediately, ensuring the session was effective. Sarah therefore carried out reflection in action.

Table 7.1 Example learning journal

Experience *significant event or incident*	Last night was the first session with a new group and I felt it didn't go well. I focused too much on what I wanted to teach and too little on how and what the group wanted to learn. Some of the learners stayed behind to ask a lot of questions that I thought I had addressed in the session, a few said they were confused and thought the programme would not meet their expectations.
Describe *who, what, when, where*	There were 16 learners aged 29 to 65 attending an evening class (accountancy for beginners) from 6–9 p.m. The session took place in a classroom with a broken projector, windows that wouldn't open and not enough chairs.
Analyse *why, how* *(impact on teaching and learning)*	I should have arrived earlier to check that the projector was working as this delayed the session by 10 minutes. I had to move some chairs from the room across the corridor and leave the door wedged open to let fresh air in. Had I sorted this out prior to the learners arriving, they would not have known of the problems. The class would then have started promptly and I would not have been flustered. I had too much paperwork to get through, the learners had to fill in an enrolment form, I needed to carry out an initial assessment of their prior learning and ascertain if anyone had any particular needs. I also wanted them to take a learning styles test but there wasn't enough time. I had a list of things I wanted to get through, including an icebreaker and agreeing the ground rules but I forgot to agree the ground rules as I was rushing things. As a result I looked unprofessional. The icebreaker went well but was a bit hurried due to the late start. I had an induction checklist which kept me focused, but it was 7.30 p.m. before I realised the learners needed a break. By this time, some of them were not paying attention to me but talking to others. I feel not much learning took place as I was focusing too much on the paperwork and programme requirements.
Revise *changes and/or improvements required*	I will arrive earlier to ensure there are enough chairs and that the projector is working. I will apologise at the beginning of next week's session and I will ask what the learners' expectations are and explain how I can meet them. We will set the ground rules next week. In future, I will interview all learners in advance and ask them to complete the enrolment form, learning styles test and an initial assessment prior to their commencing. This will help me ascertain all the information I need to help plan my first session, and make it go more smoothly. It will also ensure they are all on the right programme. I have reported the windows to the caretaker. I will allow extra time in my session plan to account for questions and answers, and ensure the focus is upon their learning rather than my teaching. I have realised the first session is not about me and the paperwork I need to complete, but about what the learners want to know and learn about the subject.

Reflection on action takes place after the incident and is a more conscious process. This allows you time to think about the incident, consider a different approach, or to talk to others about it before making changes.

Brookfield (1995) identified the importance of being critical when reflecting. He advocated four points of view when looking at practice which he called critical lenses. These lenses are from the point of view of:

- the teacher;

- the learner;

- colleagues;

- theories and literature.

Using these points makes the reflection critical, by firstly looking at it from your own point of view; secondly, how your learner perceived your actions and what they liked and disliked; thirdly, the view from colleagues; for example, your mentor is taken into consideration. This enables you to have a critical conversation about your actions which might highlight things you hadn't considered. Fourthly, you should link your reflections to theories and literature, comparing your own ideas with others.

The process of self-reflection and your own further development should help improve the quality of your delivery to your learners.

Extension Activity

Reflect upon the next session you attend or teach. Evaluate how the session went, how you reacted to situations and what you would do differently next time. Research other reflective theorists such as Gibbs' (1988) reflective cycle.

Continuing professional development

There are constant changes in education; therefore it is crucial to keep up to date with any developments. Examples include changes to the qualifications you will teach, changes to policies and practices within your organisation, regulatory requirements and government policies. Your organisation may have a strategy for continuing professional development (CPD) which will prioritise activities they consider are important to improving standards. CPD can be formal or informal, planned well in advance or be opportunistic, but should have a real impact upon your teaching role, leading to an improvement in practice.

If you are working towards Associate or Qualified Teacher Status in the Learning and Skills Sector (ATLS/QTLS), you must evidence your CPD annually. Once you have achieved your ATLS or QTLS status, you will need to maintain your Licence to Practise by partaking in relevant CPD activities, which the Institute for Learning (IfL) can monitor and sample.

Opportunities for professional development include:

- attending events and training programmes;

- attending meetings;

- e-learning activities;

- evaluating feedback from peers and learners;

- improving own skills such as maths and English;

- membership of professional associations or committees;

- observing colleagues;

- researching developments or changes to your subject and/or relevant legislation;

- secondments;

- self-reflection;

- shadowing colleagues;

- standardisation activities;

- studying for relevant qualifications;

- subscribing to and reading relevant journals and websites;

- visiting other organisations;

- voluntary work;

- work experience placements;

- writing or reviewing books and articles.

All CPD activities must be documented in some way and reflected upon. This can be via the IfL website, your organisation's systems, or your own manual or electronic record. Maintaining your CPD will ensure you are not only competent at your job role, but also up to date with the latest developments regarding your specialist subject and teaching and learning approaches.

The following websites are useful to gain up-to-date information regarding developments in the Lifelong Learning Sector.

Department for Business, Innovation and Skills – www.bis.gov.uk

Department for Education – www.education.gov.uk

Equality and Diversity Forum – www.edf.org.uk

Government updates: Education and Learning –
www.direct.gov.uk/en/EducationAndLearning/index.htm

Institute for Learning – www.ifl.ac.uk

Learning and Skills Improvement Service – www.lsis.org.uk

Lifelong Learning UK – www.lluk.org

National Institute of Adult Continuing Education – www.niace.org.uk

Ofqual – www.ofqual.gov.uk/

Times Educational Supplement Online – www.tes.co.uk

Extension Activity

Thinking about the subject you wish to teach, what do you need to do to ensure you are up to date and current with your knowledge and skills? Access the websites listed above and subscribe to any regular updates.

Progression

Before you complete your PTLLS Award, you may find it useful to summarise your learning and create an action plan or summative profile for your future development. This could be a list of your strengths and achievements so far, areas you would like to develop or improve, and how you will work towards accomplishing them. All teachers must register with the Institute for Learning (IfL) within six months of starting their job role and gain the PTLLS Award within one year. PTLLS holders will be classed as an Affiliate member until fully qualified. Membership of the IfL does not give you your teaching status; a separate process must be gone through to achieve your Licence to Practise.

After achieving the PTLLS Award, you should work towards a higher-level teaching qualification which will depend upon your job role as either an Associate or Full teacher (see Chapter 1). An Associate teacher does not carry out or have the responsibilities that a Full teacher would, i.e. they might teach programmes whereby someone else has designed the scheme of work, session plans and resources. Associate teachers must take the Certificate in Teaching in the Lifelong Learning Sector (CTLLS). Full teachers must take the Diploma in Teaching in the Lifelong Learning Sector (DTTLS), also known as the Certificate in Education or Post Graduate/Professional Certificate in Education (PGCE).

You will also need to demonstrate you have achieved the minimum core of literacy, language, numeracy and information communication technology (ICT) skills.

Once you have achieved the required qualifications, you will undertake an induction period, known as Professional Formation. This is:

> . . . the post-qualification process by which a teacher demonstrates through professional practice:
>
> 1. the ability to use effectively the skills and knowledge acquired whilst training to be a teacher;
> 2. and the capacity to meet the occupational standards required of a teacher.
>   (The Further Education Teachers' Qualifications (England) Regulations, 2007)

Once you have successfully achieved the required teaching qualifications and minimum core aspects, and completed the professional formation process, you can apply to the IfL for your teaching status and Licence to Practise. The teaching status of Associate Teacher Learning and Skills (ATLS) is for Associate teachers. Qualified Teacher Learning and Skills (QTLS) is for Full teachers and does not relate to whether you are employed part time or full time.

Extension Activity

Register with the Institute for Learning (IfL) online at www.ifl.ac.uk. You will need to have details of your teaching and specialist subject qualifications available. (This would be a good time to update your curriculum vitae and CPD record.) Have a look at the different pages on the IfL website to familiarise yourself with the process of how to gain your Licence to Practise.

Summary

In this chapter you have learnt about:

- quality assurance;
- evaluation;
- self-reflection and learning journals;
- continuing professional development;
- progression.

Theory focus

References and further information

Brookfield, SD (1995) *Becoming a Critically Reflective Teacher.* San Francisco: Jossey Bass.

Gibbs, G (1988) *Learning by Doing: A guide to teaching and learning methods.* Oxford: Further Education Unit.

Gravells, A and Simpson, S (2010) *Planning and Enabling Learning in the Lifelong Learning Sector* (2nd edn). Exeter: Learning Matters.

Schön, D (1983) *The Reflective Practitioner.* London: Temple Smith.

Wallace, S (2007) *Achieving QTLS: Teaching, tutoring and training in the Lifelong Learning Sector* (3rd edn). Exeter: Learning Matters.

Wood, J and Dickinson, J (2011) *Quality assurance and evaluation in the Lifelong Learning Sector.* Exeter: Learning Matters.

Websites

English and Maths online learning – www.move-on.org.uk

Institute for Learning (IfL) – www.ifl.ac.uk

Minimum Core – www.lluk.org/3043.htm

Introduction

In this chapter you will learn about:

- planning;
- preparing;
- delivering;
- evaluating.

This chapter will assist you in preparation for your micro-teach session. At the end of each section is an activity to help you to put theory into practice. Guidance is given for pre-service and in-service micro-teach sessions. A more detailed version of this chapter appears in *Passing PTLLS Assessments* by Ann Gravells.

This chapter contributes towards the following scope, knowledge and practice aspects of the Professional Standards for Teachers, Tutors and Trainers in the Lifelong Learning Sector:

ASI, AS4, AS7, AK7.3, API.I, AP4.I, AP4.2, AP6.2, AP7.3;
BSI, BS2, BS3, BS5, BK.2.6, BK.3.I, BK.3.2, BK.3.3, BPI.I, BPI.2, BPI.3, BP2.I, BP2.2, BP2.3, BP2.4, BP2.6, BP3.I, BP3.2, BP3.3, BP3.4, BP5.I, BP5.2;
CS2, CS4, CKI.I, CK2.I, CP2.I, CP3.I;
DSI, DS3, DKI.I, DKI.2, DKI.3, DK2.I, DK3.I, DPI.I, DPI.2, DPI.3, DP2.I, DP3.I;
ESI, ES2, ES4, EKI.I, EKI.2, EKI.3, EK2.3, EK4.2, EPI.I, EPI.2, EPI.3, EP2.I, EP2.2, EP2.3, EP4.I, EP4.2.

Planning

To achieve the PTLLS Award you need to demonstrate your skills and knowledge as a teacher. You are therefore required to plan, prepare, deliver and evaluate a short teaching session. This will either be to your peers if you are pre-service or to your current learners if you are in-service. This gives you the opportunity to put theory into practice and will usually be for a minimum of 15 or 30 minutes, the date, time and place being agreed in advance. You will be assessed by your teacher or an observer who will probably use an observation checklist, which you would find useful to see in advance. This will help you know what they are looking for and enable you to ask any questions beforehand. Your observer might make a visual recording of your session which you can view to help your evaluation process. This will enable you to see things you were not aware of; for example, saying *erm*, using a lot of hand gestures or not using enough eye contact with your learners. You should be told in advance if you are going to be recorded, try not to be put off by it, but embrace it as a way of developing yourself further.

You may find it useful to ask your observer the following questions.

- How long will my session be?
- When and where will it take place?
- Which session plan pro-forma must I use?
- When will you need to see my session plan?
- What if I change my mind about what I'm going to do?
- What equipment and resources are available to me?
- How many people will I be delivering to?
- Do I need to know their learning styles or any individual needs?
- Can I find out in advance what prior knowledge and/or experience my learners have of my subject?
- What will I need to bring with me, e.g. board markers, clock, paper?
- Can I arrive early to set up the area, e.g. move tables, check resources?
- What computer programs/versions are available?
- Should I e-mail my presentation to you or should I bring it on a memory stick?
- Is there somewhere I can get handouts photocopied in advance?
- Should I start with an icebreaker and ground rules?
- Do I need to embed functional skills?
- What kind of assessment activity should I use?
- How will I receive feedback afterwards?

You will need to create a session plan in advance which should have a clear aim (what you want your learners to achieve), which is then broken down into objectives (how your learners will achieve your aim). Your plan should show what you expect your learners to achieve expressed in a way that will enable you to assess that learning has taken place. Your observer will probably want to see your session plan well in advance to give you advice and support. See Chapter 4 for guidance regarding session planning.

Your session plan should have a beginning (the introduction), a middle section (the development) and an ending (the summary/conclusion) which should show a logical progression of learning and assessment. Timings should be allocated to each of the teaching and learning activities you plan to use in each section.

Preparing

Once you have your session plan, you will need to design all the activities, handouts, resources, presentations and assessment activities you intend to use. You may need to learn how to use something in advance; for example, if you wish to use a computerised presentation during your session. You should check all presentations and documents for spelling, grammar and punctuation errors and ensure text and pictures represent all aspects of equality and diversity. If you are delivering a 30-minute session and you plan to show a video for ten minutes, this will not demonstrate how teaching and learning are taking place. Videos are good for visual learners, but if used, keep them short or you may lose the attention of other learners.

Carry out a trial run with friends or family to check your timings. You might find that what you planned to cover in 30 minutes takes only 20. Time will go quickly during your micro-teach session, particularly if you are asked lots of questions. Make sure you have all the necessary equipment, resources and stationery. A clock or a watch in a visible place will help you keep track of time. Try to have a contingency plan in case anything goes wrong, for example, a hard copy of an electronic presentation.

If possible check in advance and/or arrive early to see that everything is available and working in the room you will be in. You may want to rearrange the area beforehand to suit your subject and to enable everyone to see and hear you. Time for setting up and clearing away afterwards should be outside of your observed time. You may need two copies of your session plan, one for yourself and one for your observer.

Delivering

The micro-teach is a learning experience and a chance to put all your new-found theory into practice. You may feel nervous as you will be observed. However, try to imagine you are playing a role and this should help your confidence. You are the teacher in this situation; you need to be in control and not let any personal issues affect you. If you are organised and have checked the room and equipment in advance, hopefully you won't encounter any problems. Try to relax, but stay focused and above all enjoy yourself. As you will have prepared your session plan carefully, your delivery should follow logically through the introduction, development and summary stages.

Introduction

Before you speak, take a few deep breaths, smile at your learners and use eye contact; this should help you to relax. Begin by introducing yourself, your aim and objectives. You might like to keep these on display throughout your session – perhaps on a piece of flipchart paper on the wall. Don't tell your learners that you are nervous as it probably won't show. Stand tall and speak a little louder and slower than normal as being anxious or nervous may make you speak faster. If you feel you are shaking, it is highly likely no one will notice. If your mind suddenly goes blank, take a couple of deep breaths for a few seconds and look at your session plan to help you refocus; it might seem a long time to you but it won't to your learners. You will need to establish a rapport with your learners and engage and interact with them from the start. Asking the question *Has anyone done this before?* is a good way of involving your learners in your subject and helps you check any prior learning.

Keep your session plan handy as a prompt. If you feel you might forget something, use a highlight pen beforehand to mark key words which you can quickly look at. Use eye contact with all your learners and standing rather than sitting will help your confidence and voice projection. Keep things simple, don't try to deliver too much material, or expect too much from your learners – your subject may be very new to them. If this is the first time you have met your learners, you might want to carry out a short icebreaker with them or ask them to introduce themselves to you. You may not have time to agree any ground rules; however, you could state that you expect mobile phones to be switched off. You might like to encourage your learners to ask questions if they need to clarify any points.

Development

You should use a variety of teaching and learning approaches to reach all learning styles and to retain motivation. Summarise and recap regularly to reinforce points, and ask open questions to check knowledge. Try to use names when talking to your learners and if possible address everyone in the group; don't just focus on a particular learner who you know can give you the correct answers. Having your learners' names written down in advance will help.

The timing of activities needs to be followed carefully; if you are delivering only a 15-minute session you may not have time for group activities. If you do set activities, think what you will be doing while your learners are working; moving around the room and observing or asking questions shows you are in control. Longer sessions benefit from a mixture of teaching and learning approaches to ensure all learning styles will be met.

Summary

A short quiz or multiple-choice test towards the end of your session is a good way to check knowledge if you have time, and acts as an assessment activity. Your summary should recap your aim and objectives. You might like to ask your learners if they have any questions. However, you may be met with silence, or they might have lots of questions which will then impede upon your time. If you find you have covered everything and have spare time, you could ask each member of the group to state one thing they feel they have learnt from the session. This is a good way of filling in spare time if necessary, and shows you what each learner has learnt. You could prepare a handout in advance which summarises your session and this could be given at the end. If you issue it during the session your learners will look at it and not you.

If you are unsure of how to end your session, simply say *Thank you*; this will indicate to your group you have finished. Make sure you leave the area tidy afterwards.

Pre-service micro-teach session

As a pre-service teacher you will be delivering to a group of your peers who will become your learners for the session. This might be the first time you have taught a group of people and your peers will probably be very encouraging and supportive. If you have chosen to deliver a subject you know well, your knowledge should help your confidence. You will probably be in the same environment you have been learning in, or a central meeting point if you have been studying through a distance-learning programme. Hopefully you will have met your peers previously and feel comfortable delivering to them; if not, it would be useful to talk to them beforehand to help everyone relax. If you are due to deliver after someone else, you will probably be thinking about your own micro-teach session rather than focusing upon theirs. Try not to do this as it may make you more nervous. Being well prepared and having self-confidence and knowledge of your subject should help alleviate any worries.

In-service teaching session

You might be required to deliver your session to your peers rather than to your own learners. If this is the case, please read the pre-service section above. However, delivering to your peer group would be a good time to try out something different or new in a safe environment, rather than repeating a session you would normally deliver to your own learners.

You might already have some experience of teaching, therefore delivering a session to your own learners should be fairly straightforward. Your session might last longer than the time your observer will be present, they might therefore miss the beginning or ending and arrive part way through. You should try to plan the session to allow time to talk to your observer either before or afterwards. This will enable you to discuss your delivery, justify any aspects they have missed and to receive feedback. The session you are delivering may be one of many, for which you will have a scheme of work to follow. You may want to introduce the observer to the group and state they are observing you, not them. Having a stranger in the room might lead to some behaviour issues. If so, you must deal with these as soon as they arise and in a professional manner.

Activity

Imagine the group you will deliver your micro-teach session to is made up of the following: six females and eight males aged between 16 and 65, from a variety of backgrounds. Three are unemployed, one is dyslexic and one is a wheelchair user. Learning styles are: nine kinaesthetic, two visual, two read/write and one aural. What adaptations would you make to your session plan to ensure you differentiate for individual needs and included everyone in the session?

Evaluating

After your delivery you may find that your observer asks you how you felt it went before giving feedback. This will enable you to consider what went well and what you could have done differently. You should receive oral feedback along with a completed assessment checklist from your observer. You might also receive feedback from your peers which can be used to inform your self-evaluation process. Once you have finished your micro-teach session, you might be so relieved or busy packing away that you don't fully take on board what is being said to you. Listen carefully and ask questions to clarify any points you are unsure of. Try not to interrupt or become defensive when receiving feedback and don't take anything personally – the feedback will be given to help you improve.

Evaluating your delivery is an important aspect of your learning and development and you may need to complete a self-evaluation form to formalise this. You might think you have done really well, but you may have received some helpful advice during the feedback process which could help you improve further.

When evaluating yourself, consider your strengths, areas for development and any action and improvements required from a teaching perspective as well as your subject knowledge. Hopefully, you enjoyed your micro-teach session and it has confirmed you do want to have a career as a teacher. However, the experience might have made you think that teaching just isn't for you at this point in time. Conversely it might make you more determined to improve and develop further.

Activity

After you have delivered your role-play micro-teach and received feedback, evaluate your strengths and areas for development. Did you achieve your aim effectively? Did your learners achieve the objectives? Analyse the effectiveness of the resources you used and consider what you would change or modify for your actual micro-teach session.

Summary

In this chapter you have learnt about:

- planning;

- preparing;

- delivering;

- evaluating.

Theory focus

References and further information

Duckworth, V, Wood, J, Bostock, J and Dickinson, J (2010) *Successful Teaching Practice in the Lifelong Learning Sector*. Exeter: Learning Matters.

Gravells, A (2010) *Passing PTLLS Assessments*. Exeter: Learning Matters.

Websites

Oxford Learning Institute – Giving and receiving feedback – www.learning.ox. ac.uk/rsv.php?page=319

Unit title: Preparing to Teach in the Lifelong Learning Sector
Level: 3
Credit value: 6

Learning outcomes The learner will:	Assessment criteria The learner can:
1. Understand own role, responsibilities and boundaries of role in relation to teaching	1.1 Explain own role and responsibilities, and boundaries of own role as a teacher 1.2 Identify key aspects of relevant current legislative requirements and codes of practice within a specific context 1.3 Identify other points of referral available to meet the potential needs of learners 1.4 Identify issues of equality and diversity, and ways to promote inclusion 1.5 Explain the need for record keeping
2. Understand appropriate teaching and learning approaches in the specialist area	2.1 Identify and demonstrate relevant approaches to teaching and learning in relation to the specialist area 2.2 Explain ways to embed elements of functional skills in the specialist area 2.3 Justify selection of teaching and learning approaches for a specific session
3. Demonstrate session planning skills	3.1 Plan a teaching and learning session which meets the needs of individual learners 3.2 Justify selection of resources for a specific session
4. Understand how to deliver inclusive sessions which motivate learners	4.1 Explain ways to establish ground rules with learners which underpin appropriate behaviour and respect for others 4.2 Use a range of appropriate and effective teaching and learning approaches to engage and motivate learners 4.3 Explain and demonstrate good practice in giving feedback 4.4 Communicate appropriately and effectively with learners 4.5 Reflect on and evaluate the effectiveness of own teaching
5. Understand the use of different assessment methods and the need for record keeping	5.1 Identify different assessment methods 5.2 Explain the use of assessment methods in different contexts, including reference to initial assessment 5.3 Explain the need for record keeping in relation to assessment

Unit title: Preparing to Teach in the Lifelong Learning Sector
Level: 4
Credit value: 6

Learning outcomes The learner will:	Assessment criteria The learner can:
1. Understand own role, responsibilities and boundaries of role in relation to teaching	1.1 Review own role and responsibilities, and boundaries of own role as a teacher 1.2 Summarise key aspects of relevant current legislative requirements and codes of practice within a specific context 1.3 Review other points of referral available to meet the potential needs of learners 1.4 Discuss issues of equality and diversity, and ways to promote inclusion 1.5 Justify the need for record keeping
2. Understand appropriate teaching and learning approaches in the specialist area	2.1 Identify, adapt and use relevant approaches to teaching and learning in relation to the specialist area 2.2 Evaluate a range of ways to embed elements of functional skills in the specialist area 2.3 Evaluate the teaching and learning approaches for a specific session
3. Demonstrate session planning skills	3.1 Plan a teaching and learning session which meets the needs of individual learners 3.2 Evaluate how the planned session meets the needs of individual learners 3.3 Analyse the effectiveness of the resources for a specific session
4. Understand how to deliver inclusive sessions which motivate learners	4.1 Analyse different ways to establish ground rules with learners which underpin appropriate behaviour and respect for others 4.2 Use a range of appropriate and effective teaching and learning approaches to engage and motivate learners 4.3 Explain different methods of giving feedback 4.4 Demonstrate good practice in giving feedback 4.5 Communicate appropriately and effectively with learners 4.6 Reflect on and evaluate the effectiveness of own teaching, making recommendations for modification as appropriate
5. Understand the use of different assessment methods and the need for record keeping	5.1 Review a range of different assessment methods 5.2 Evaluate the use of assessment methods in different contexts, including reference to initial assessment 5.3 Justify the need for record keeping in relation to assessment

Teaching and learning checklist
Identifying needs
Do I...?

- [ ] Know who I will be teaching, i.e. details of all learners and any specific requirements
- [ ] Know anything about the learners that might affect my teaching or their learning
- [ ] Need to carry out an initial assessment or diagnostic test with learners
- [ ] Need to carry out a learning styles test with learners
- [ ] Need to agree an action plan or individual learning plan with learners
- [ ] Need to learn anything myself before I can teach the subject
- [ ] Know the organisational policies such as health and safety, equality and diversity, safeguarding, etc., and carry out any risk assessments or necessary checks

Planning learning
Do I...?

- [ ] Have a syllabus or qualification handbook
- [ ] Have an induction checklist
- [ ] Need to create a scheme of work which shows a logical progression of learning
- [ ] Need to create a session plan
- [ ] Have clear aims and SMART objectives
- [ ] Know when and where I will be teaching, to how many and for how long
- [ ] Need to prepare the learning environment
- [ ] Need a clock or watch to keep track of time
- [ ] Need to book or obtain any specialist equipment or resources
- [ ] Need to know any organisational procedures, e.g. fire exits, accidents, appeals
- [ ] Need to find out where facilities are, such as catering, toilets
- [ ] Need to arrange refreshments, transport or parking
- [ ] Need to send out any pre-programme information and/or inform reception staff where to direct learners
- [ ] Need to devise suitable learning activities, resources and assessments and get these photocopied
- [ ] Need to check spelling, grammar and punctuation of presentations and handouts
- [ ] Have a contingency plan in case anything goes wrong, and extra activities if needed

Enabling learning
Can I...?

- [ ] Ensure the environment is suitable, e.g. heating, lighting, ventilation, seating arrangements and disability access
- [ ] Arrive early to set up and check equipment, obtain resources, etc.
- [ ] Complete any necessary administrative requirements, e.g. register
- [ ] Introduce the session aims and objectives
- [ ] Recap the previous session (if applicable)
- [ ] Use an icebreaker, energiser or starter activity
- [ ] Negotiate ground rules
- [ ] Stipulate the times of breaks

- [ ] Use a variety of teaching and learning approaches, activities and resources to include and differentiate for all learners, taking into account equality and diversity
- [ ] Mix formal and informal teaching in an appropriate manner
- [ ] Embed Functional Skills, Equality and Diversity and the Every Child Matters outcomes
- [ ] Manage behaviour and disruption as it occurs
- [ ] Take any additional learner needs into consideration and support learners as necessary
- [ ] Leave personal problems behind and act professional at all times
- [ ] Prepare an extension activity for learners who finish tasks earlier than others, or need challenging further
- [ ] Allow time for questions
- [ ] Summarise the session and recap aims and objectives (or learning outcomes)
- [ ] Leave the venue tidy
- [ ] Maintain all relevant records

Assessing learning
Can I...?
- [ ] Ensure the validity and reliability of all assessment methods
- [ ] Ask open questions to check knowledge
- [ ] Assess learners on an individual basis – formally and informally
- [ ] Give feedback to learners on an individual basis in a constructive manner
- [ ] Review learner progress, e.g. through tutorials
- [ ] Keep records of progress and assessment decisions

Quality assurance and Evaluation
Did I...?
- [ ] Deliver an introduction, main content and summary
- [ ] Follow the timings on the session plan; if not, what would I change and why
- [ ] Establish and maintain a rapport, putting learners at ease
- [ ] Project energy, enthusiasm and passion
- [ ] Have a structured approach
- [ ] Remain in control and deal with any difficult or unexpected situations appropriately
- [ ] Appear confident and professional with a positive attitude
- [ ] Use eye contact with all learners
- [ ] Use individual names
- [ ] Fidget or fiddle with anything, if so, how could I stop
- [ ] Listen actively
- [ ] Dress and act appropriately
- [ ] Answer questions appropriately
- [ ] Recap key points regularly
- [ ] Use appropriate body language and non-verbal communication
- [ ] Limit the use of jargon or acronyms
- [ ] Achieve the aim enabling the learners to achieve their objectives
- [ ] Provide opportunities for learner feedback
- [ ] Enjoy the session; if not, why not
- [ ] Follow all regulations and codes of practice
- [ ] Reflect on the session content, along with the teaching and learning process to make improvements for the future

Added to a page number 'f' denotes a figure and 't' denotes a table.

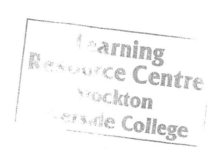